Reflections on Faith & History

by

Dr. Milton C. Sernett

Dedicated to the Members of the Cazenovia United Methodist Church and the Nelson United Methodist Church—Past and Present

©2016
Cazenovia, New York

CONTENTS

Preface   7

Section I   Cazenovia   9

Moments in the History of Methodism in Cazenovia
Ministers of the Church
A Selected Chronology

Section II   Nelson   39

A Brief History of Methodism in Nelson
Ministers of the Church
A Selected Chronology

Section III   REFLECTIONS   49

October 2011   Thoughts for Reformation Sunday
November 2011   On the Art of Giving Thanks
December 2011   The Christmas Cow Is Missing!

January 2012   Do You Have a Storm Home for 2012?
February 2012   Thin Ice!
March 2012   Looking for a Good Woman?
April 2012   Come, Walk with Me!
May 2012   To the Ladies that Sew
June 2012   "Fare Thee Well"
July 2012   On Reaching the Half Century Mark-**twenty years later!**
August 2012   The Hat
September 2012   What Makes You Special?
October 2012   A Short Course in Christian Continuing Education
November 2012   On Being the Apple of God's Eye
December 2012   An Old Story Retold

January 2013	Looking for Happiness in the New Year?
February 2013	God's Shoe Box of Love
March 2013	Highway to Heaven
April 2013	Warble On!
May 2013	Go Fish!
June 2013	"Let Us Cross Over the River and Rest"
July 2013	An Uplifting Experience!
August 2013	Searching for Love
September 2013	Who's Been Sitting in My Pew?
October 2013	"His Master's Voice"
November 2013	"With Malice Toward None"
December 2013	How to Avoid Eileschpijjel's Christmas
January 2014	Free and Clear!
February 2014	Taking Inventory
March 2014	Pure Christianity & New York Grade A Light Amber
April 2014	Easter's Musical Olympics
May 2014	In Memorium
June 2014	"Dominus Baseball"
July 2014	The Way Home
August 2014	Smile! You're on God's Time
September 2014	"Teacher, Teacher . . ."
October 2014	Christian Croquet, Anyone?
November 2014	Ragamuffin
December 2014	To Truss a Goose
January 2015	Finding Your Way in 2015
February 2015	"He Belongs to The Angels, Now"
March 2015	Keep Your Fork!
April 2015	Your Easter Compass
May 2015	Mud in May, and Other Simple Gospel Pleasures
June 2015	On the Power of Prayer
July 2015	"The Magnificent Sanctuary Band"
August 2015	Call Forwarding
September 2015	The Sweet Sleep of Labor
October 2015	The Tablecloth

November 2015   Egg Money
December 2015   My Fiji Christmas

January 2016   It's a Windy Day!
February 2016   Where's Your Comfort Blanket?
March 2016   The Voice of the Turtle Dove on Easter Morning
April 2016   Celestial Humor
May 2016   In Memorium
June 2016   Roots and Reunions
July 2016   Keeping Cool
August 2016   On Why There Are No Cell Phones in Heaven
September 2016   Home Schooling

About the Author   195

Preface . . .

My wife Jan and I began attending Cazenovia's First United Methodist Church in 2011. We lived on Ridge Road about four miles north of this assembly of Christians and wanted a place of worship closer to home than Cicero's Faith Lutheran Church, in which we had been active since 1975. We became associate members of the Methodist congregation in Cazenovia on February 2, 2013. This allowed us to remain on the roster of Faith Lutheran and at the same time establish a Methodist connection. Cazenovia's First United Methodist Church is a joint parish with the Nelson United Methodist Church.

The United Methodist Church is a Protestant denomination that came about in 1968 when The Methodist Church and The Evangelical United Brethren Church merged into one religious body. Both religious traditions have much older histories. Methodism (sometimes known as Wesleyanism) began in England during the 18th-century under the leadership of John Wesley who attempted to reform the Anglican church from within. The Brethren movement has roots in 18-century Europe, especially Germany.

When we were regularly attending Faith Lutheran Church in Cicero, New York, I started in 1979 to write a monthly "Reflections" essay for the church newsletter. In November 2011, I started to write similar essays, food for the soul as it were, on a monthly basis for folks who attended services at the Cazenovia United Methodist Church and the Nelson United Methodist Church. This volume is a collection of those essays. I have also included seven historical articles on the history of Methodism in Cazenovia. Originally submitted for publication in a series called "Moments in Methodism" in The Cazenovia Republican, the articles are reproduced here in slightly revised form.

The historical information on the Nelson United Methodist Church was provided by Fay Lyon. The Cazenovia and Nelson congregations became one parish in 1993 (along with the Erieville church). The Erieville congregation left in 2003. The Cazenovia and Nelson churches continue as one parish giving witness to the Christian faith and ministry.

Dr. Milt Sernett

Cazenovia United Methodist Church
21 Lincklaen St.
Cazenovia, NY 13035
Phone:
315-655-8014
E-mail:
caznelson@windstream.net

Nelson United Methodist Church
3333 Route 20 East
Cazenovia, NY 13035

Parish website:
http://www.cazenovianelsonumchurch.org

Section I: CAZENOVIA

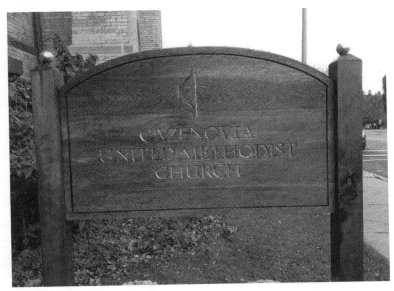

Photos courtesy of Pastor Kevin McAllister

Photo courtesy of Pastor Kevin McAllister

Photo courtesy of Jason Emerson

Methodism in Cazenovia

by

Dr. Milton C. Sernett

I. Early History of Methodism in Cazenovia

Having taught history at Syracuse University for three decades until retiring in 2005, I have a special interest in local history and am proud to call Cazenovia home, though we live outside the village limits. In the interests of full disclosure, I am equally proud to say that my wife and I are "associate members" of the Cazenovia United Methodist Church, though we have retained our Lutheran identities, forged since childhood in the Midwest. Curiously enough, there is presently no Lutheran church in Madison County, nor has there ever been, as far as I know.

Imagine yourself to be a weary traveler on a horse-drawn coach arriving at the Lincklaen House in 1836. You are hungry and thirsty, of course. The hostellers of the Lincklaen House will serve you well. But what if you needed spiritual sustenance? What did Cazenovia, then with about 240 dwellings, have to offer? According to Thomas F. Gordon's Gazetteer of the State of New York (published in 1836), there were four churches (1 Presbyterian, 1 Congregational, 1 Methodist, and 1 Baptist). The Village of Cazenovia was then about sixteen years old, having been incorporated in 1810, though its founding is usually dated to c. 1795 due to the efforts of Col. John Lincklaen, agent of the Holland Land Company.

If you, the traveler, were from New England, rooted in the old Puritan or Calvinist culture, you likely would have sought out Cazenovia's First Presbyterian Church. Built in 1806 on the north side of the Green, the church was moved to its present location on Albany Street in 1828. Presbyterians, especially when pastored by the formidable Reverend Mr. Leonard, generally thought of themselves as belonging to a higher social class than Baptists who ranked above the upstart Methodists, whose proclivity for enthusiastic or demonstrative worship troubled the more sedate Presbyterians. Cazenovia Baptists organized themselves into a church in 1815 as a "daughter congregation" of the Baptist society in New Woodstock. The First Free Congregational Society began in 1834.

Let us assume that you are the Methodist religious persuasion in 1836. Once you have supped and perhaps rested at the Lincklaen House, itself a new structure open to travelers on the Cherry Valley Turnpike (designated U. S. Route 20 in 1926), you needed only walk up Lincklaen Street (then unpaved) to find Cazenovia's Methodist church at the corner of Lincklaen and Seminary. The Methodists were then worshipping in what became known as the Old Stone Church, though in 1836 it was but four years "old." The present brick edifice designed by the famous Syracuse architect, Archimedes A. Russell was erected in 1872.

Methodists in Cazenovia first banded together in 1816. Initially, so we are led to believe, these Methodists, not having much in the way of worldly goods to put up their own house of worship, met in an old distillery east of the village. This must have been galling, to say the least, for most Methodists held temperance principles and abhorred the use and abuse of alcoholic beverages. When the Madison County Courthouse, then located on the grounds of today's Cazenovia College, went up for sale in 1819, the Methodists outbid the Baptists for the building, paying $1810. But being men and women of very modest means, the Methodists were unable to keep up the mortgage by subscription and sold the two story brick building to the Genesee Conference of the Methodist Episcopal Church in 1823 for use as a place for instruction and chapel worship by the newly founded Genesee Conference Seminary.

The Seminary was not, as the name might imply, a theological training institution for men on the path to becoming ordained elders in the Methodist Church, but a non-sectarian academy for young men and women, neither high school nor college in the sense those appellations are understood today, but a sort of hybrid.

Cazenovia Methodists, including members of the Seminary faculty and like-minded students, used the chapel of the Seminary for worship for a number of years, until building the Stone Church in 1832.

II. George W. Peck, Early Methodist Pastor in Cazenovia

George W. Peck authored a series of newspaper articles and books beginning in 1871 about a naughty boy. These humorous stories about "Peck's Bad Boy" inspired a movie in 1934 with Jackie Cooper playing the miscreant youth. The George Peck of which I write, however, is not the author of fictional works but the American Methodist Episcopal clergyman who once served as President of Cazenovia Seminary and as pastor of the Cazenovia Methodist Society when the Stone Church was erected in 1832.

The Rev. George Peck (1797-1876) was one of the famous five Peck brothers, sons of the Rev. Luther Peck. All became Methodist ministers. George's brother, the Rev. Jesse Truesdell Peck, became a Methodist Bishop and was the first Chairman of Syracuse University's Board of Trustees. Syracuse University's Peck Hall (601 East Genesee Street) is named in his honor. The George Peck Papers are in the Special Collections Research Center of the Syracuse University Library. The collection includes George Peck's correspondence, financial papers, publications, and miscellaneous memorabilia such as his eyeglasses, a leather pouch, a pen wiper, and, curiously, various seeds.

Born in 1797 at Middlefield, New York, George Peck became licensed as a local Methodist preacher in 1816. He married Mary Meyers in 1819. The couple had four children, two of whom (George M. Peck and Luther Wesley Peck) became Methodists ministers like their father. George and May Peck had one daughter, Mary Helen, who became the mother of the author Stephen Crane (1871-1900), most famous for his book The Red Badge of Courage. Crane attended but did not graduate from Syracuse University, then a Methodist school. Of the proclivity of male members of the Peck side of his family tree to become Methodist ministers, Crane said: "Upon my mother's side, everyone in my family became a Methodist clergyman as soon as they could walk, the ambling-nag, saddlebag, exhorting kind."

Crane's maternal grandfather, the Rev. George Peck, rode his horse as an itinerant Methodist preacher on various circuits in Central New York. He conducted camp meetings and revivals and tried to plant the flag of Methodism in places not far removed from frontier conditions as well as in cities such as Utica. He preached against the intemperate use of alcohol and, though often sick from his strenuous labors in both heat and cold, he ministered to families in great need of spiritual care.

The Oneida Conference appointed Peck to Cazenovia in 1831. Peck recalled: "Our congregations filled the Seminary Chapel [the old Madison County Courthouse], in which all our religious services were held . . . The teachers and students of the Seminary formed a large part of the audience at every meeting."

Anxious to have a place to worship of their own, the leaders of the Methodist Society of Cazenovia decided to put up a church building separate from Cazenovia Seminary. They circulated a subscription wherein members promised to pay specified amounts over time. This failed. The Rev. George Peck suggested a plan of selling the pews in what would become the Stone Church. He drew up "a diagram of the audience room," numbered the pews, and set up an auction. The auction resulted in proceeds sufficient to cover half of the projected cost. Reappointed in 1832 to Cazenovia, Peck preached one of the three sermons heard on Christmas Day 1832 when the Stone Church was dedicated. A "protracted meeting" or revival followed and the Stone Church gleaned "a large number" of new members, many of them students from Cazenovia Seminary.

Peck left Cazenovia in 1834, having been appointed to a Methodist Church in Auburn, but he returned in 1835, no longer as an itinerant preacher, but now as the head of Cazenovia Seminary. He reports that during his three-year tenure the Seminary generally "had good order and attention to study." Peck did ask for the expulsion of a student who refused to apologize for reading an essay the student had written disparaging revivals. Twelve to fifteen sympathizers, Peck tells us, escorted the expelled youth "to the gate, where a sleigh, drawn by four horses decorated with ribbons, received them, and they drove two or three times around the square, carrying a flag, and cheering as they passed the seminary." Peck tells us that the excitement was soon over, though one of the sympathizers also had to be expelled, "and the infidel club came to an end."

More problematic to Peck and to American Methodism in general was "the slavery question." Of that we will write in the next installment.

III. The Abolition and Slavery Controversy

John Wesley (1703-1791), the founder of Methodism in England, famously said in his tract <u>Thoughts Upon Slavery</u> (1774):

Give liberty to whom liberty is due, that is, to every child of man, to every partaker of human nature. Let none serve you but by his own act and deed, by his own voluntary action. Away with all whips, all chains, all compulsions. Be gentle toward all men; and see that you invariably do with every one as you would he should do unto you.

American Methodists became ensnared in the controversy over slavery within a few years after the demand by the abolitionist William Lloyd Garrison in 1831 for immediate, unconditional, and uncompensated abolition. The Rev. George Peck, President of Cazenovia Seminary, tells us that "the antislavery excitement in our Church reached a fearful height" in 1835. Abolitionist-minded Methodist clergymen such as La Roy Sunderland, Orange Scott, and George Storrs, most of them from New England, led the crusade to purge American Methodism of the sin of slavery. Southern Methodists fought back, arguing that slavery was merely a civil institution and not religious matter and that an attack upon slavery was an assault upon them.

Peck found himself in a precarious position, as were other moderates who tried to preserve denominational harmony. Personally, he abhorred slavery, as many British Methodists did. "Slavery," Peck affirmed, "tends to make the master-race bold, arrogant, conceited, savage, unscrupulous, and remorseless. He who would uphold it must neither fear God nor regard man." When Cazenovia Seminary president, Peck consented to the formation of a student Abolition Society and allowed public debates "on the comparative claims of the abolitionist and colonization societies." Colonizationists believed that the solution to the slavery question was the removal of African Americans to Africa. Providing an opportunity to discuss the most contentious issue of the time had, Peck recalled, "a good effect among the students, and we had no further uneasiness on the subject."

No amount of administrative wisdom could resolve the national debate among Methodists. The Southern wing of the denomination

The famous antislavery medallion created by Josiah Wedgwood, the British potter and abolitionist.

demanded that the General Conference, the supreme governing body of the church, throw out the abolitionist agitators and endorse the institution of slavery. Families and local congregations split during the bitter debate. As a member, secretary, and eventually chair of the Committee on Slavery of his denomination, Peck found himself at the center of the conflict.

The tinderbox of debate ignited at the General Conference of 1844 held in New York City when it was discovered that Bishop James O. Andrew of Georgia owned slaves. He argued that he had inherited them from his first and second wives and that he personally had "neither bought or sold a slave." Northern Methodists, even those of the moderate persuasion, could not stomach a slave-holding bishop, as bishops were supposedly to serve the entire church. American Methodism split in 1845 along sectional lines. The Methodist Episcopal Church, South did not rejoin its northern counterpart until 1939. The historian C. C. Goen has described the breakup of American Methodism along regional lines as a premonition of the Civil War--"broken churches, broken nation."

Northern Methodists were themselves divided. The radical segment, led by Orange Scott and La Roy Sunderland, formed the Wesleyan Methodist Connection (later called The Wesleyan Church) in 1841, a thoroughly abolitionist denomination. Local congregations affiliated with the Wesleyans existed in Central New York. The church in downtown Syracuse (now the Mission Restaurant at 304 E. Onondaga St.) is famous for the discovery of those clay "faces" sculpted, allegedly, by travelers on the Underground Railroad. The Rev. Luther Lee, the church's pastor, was a zealous abolitionist. The Wesleyan Church in Seneca Falls hosted the first Women's Rights Convention in 1848.

The Rev. George Peck, his three years as President of Cazenovia Seminary completed, was serving a Methodist congregation in Auburn when he tangled with Gerrit Smith, one of the nation's most outspoken abolitionists. The Peterboro reformer had publically charged, to quote Peck, "that the Methodist Church was a rum-drinking pro-slavery Church." Peck took to the columns of the Auburn Banner to answer Smith, and the two men carried on a public debate via the newspaper for brief while. Eventually, according to Peck, Smith "admitted, in his final article, that he had been misinformed as to our true position."

Gerrit Smith may have backed off from his broadside against all Methodists, but he carried on a long crusade to rid northern denominations of both open and covert pro-slavery sentiment. Smith was a leader in the "free church" movement, leaving the Presbyterian congregation in Peterboro to found a "free church" composed entirely of abolitionists. Cazenovia had its own "free church." The Free Congregational Church of Cazenovia, located where the present Catherine Cummings Theatre is, was a haven for abolitionist-minded Christians in the village.

Gerrit Smith figured prominently in the Great Cazenovia Fugitive Slave Law Convention, August 21 and 22, 1850. Along with Frederick Douglass and other abolitionists, Smith endorsed a stinging indictment of the impending Fugitive Slave Bill. A boulder and bronze marker have been placed on Sullivan Street at the location of the convention (now 9 Sullivan Street), held in the apple orchard of Grace Wilson, a Cazenovia schoolteacher. Anyone interested in learning more of the multi-faced reform career of Smith need only visit the Gerrit Smith Estate in

Peterboro, New York. It is a National Historic Landmark (www.gerritsmith.org). Visitors should also spend time there at the National Abolition Hall of Fame & Museum (www.abolitionhof.org).

Though the local Cazenovia Methodist church did not split over the issue of slavery, the Civil War dealt a cruel hand to the worshippers in the Stone Church at the corner of Lincklaen and Seminary. Though the Trustees' records do not give us specific names, we can surmise that some families lost fathers and sons on the battlefields and that members agonized over the fate of a nation so bitterly divided. After the war was over, however, thoughts turned to building a new church. More of that and of the famous architect who designed the yellow brick structure erected in 1872 that still stands comes in our next installment.

IV. Building the 1872 Yellow Brick Church

After three decades of using the Old Stone Church as a place of worship, the Methodists of Cazenovia decided to build a new and larger church. Demolition of the 1832 stone church began in April 1872. I find it fitting that the Old Stone Church, after forty years of faithful service, did not come down easily. A group of men using a rope tried to pull down the west wall, failed to do so, and it had to be dismantled brick by brick.

The Methodist trustees hoped to put up a new church at a cost not to exceed $25,000. Not surprisingly, the final outlay for the building and furnishings, including the organ, amounted to more--an estimated $35,350. With protracted legal wrangling with contractors and difficulty in funding the new church, the congregation did not become financially stable until the mid-1880s.

The Methodists chose the noted Syracuse architect Archimedes Russell (1840-1915) to draw up plans for the new church. Professor of Architecture at Syracuse University from 1873 through 1881, Russell is credited with designing more than 850 civic and commercial buildings during an extremely productive

career. A mountain of a man standing at six feet and four inches tall and weighing as much as 300 pounds, Russell designed equally monumental buildings. I offer but a short list: Crouse College, Syracuse University (1881); Third National Bank in Syracuse (1885); Central Technical High School in Syracuse (1900); and the Onondaga County Courthouse at Columbus Circle (1904-1907). It should be noted that the architectural firm of King and King, founded in 1868 in Syracuse, is still in business today. Its roots trace back to Russell's day.

Russell's architectural talents were displayed in a host of churches, as diverse in appearance as the mission-inspired architecture of the First English Lutheran Church (1911) at the corner of James Street and Townsend Street in Syracuse and the decorative English Gothic style of Saint Lucy's Roman Catholic Church (1873) on Gifford Street in Syracuse. Perhaps the hallmark of Russell's work was his eclectic and practical style.

Russell's plans called for the church to face north (toward Cazenovia Seminary. Because of the design's footprint and the inability of the Methodists to purchase the lane west of the Old Stone Church, the new church could not face east as the Old Stone Church had. Quite a few members expressed displeasure with the northern orientation. To appease them, Russell added an entrance door on the eastern side of the new structure (facing today's post office).

The laying of the cornerstone took place on July 4, 1872. The new structure, generally called the Yellow Brick Church, was built in the Romanesque Revival style with twin towers, the tallest one containing the village clock and the bell. The stone for the foundation came from a quarry in Manlius. The native yellow brick came from Cazenovia. The new church was flagged with limestone from Fulton. The main auditorium or sanctuary was said to be able to accommodate one thousand people. Beautiful stained glass windows, still to be seen today, adorned the sanctuary that at night was lit by oil chandeliers. Dedication services were conducted on December 17, 1873, with a large crowd in attendance

In subsequent years many renovations were to be made to the Yellow Brick Church. Extensive improvements took place in 1924 when the Rev. R. DeWitt Stanley was pastor. Here are a few--new roof, repairing the stained glass windows, a new vapor heating plant, replacing some of the brown stone trimmings on the exterior and painting the trim, new toilets and lavatories, a new kitchen and dining room, rewiring and improvements in lighting, and the installation of something called "the Acousticon," which I take to be a 1920s version of today's hearing aid, though these were attached and available in the pews for worshippers who had difficulty hearing.

Though the congregation settled into a new place of worship in 1873, they did so with a few reminders of their beloved Stone Church. Several of the numbered pews from the old church were placed in the new church. Wood from some of the old pews was used to construct the doors of a cabinet that was placed in the new church's Sunday School room. That cabinet remains for visitors and worshippers to see today. Most significantly, the old church bell and the village clock found a new home in the taller of the two towers that adorned the Yellow Brick Church. We will write of the strange odyssey of the bell, the clock, and the towers and their spires in our next installment.

V. Musings on the Clock, Bell, and Towers

When the clock mechanism fashioned from brass was placed in the spire of Cazenovia's Methodist Church in 1874, it was said to keep accurate time within fifteen minutes for an entire year, assuming that it was wound once a week. Russell Oechsle, an expert on historic tower clocks, has praised the Stone & Marshall built clock as "one of America's most beautiful town clocks."

Cazenovia was once the home of a guild of noteworthy clock makers. For nearly forty-five years, these skilled craftsmen created masterpieces that kept the time of day and, in most cases, tolled the hours. Our school of expert tower clockmakers began with Jehiel Clark, Sr., who passed on his business to his son Jehiel Clark, Jr., upon retirement in 1846. The Clarks created Cazenovia's old "iron town clock" that was originally placed in the tower of the Presbyterian Church in our village. The younger Clark relinquished his clock making shop to Austin W. Van Riper in 1850. Riper's machine and blacksmith shop, located along Chittenango Creek, built so many tower clocks that The Cazenovia Republican could make the claim that by 1859 every state in the Union had at least one Van Riper tower clock. That same year Van Riper died. Justice W. Marshall and John J. Stone then took over Cazenovia's tower clock making business. Milton Card joined the firm in 1870.

Van Riper and his top mechanics, John Stone and Justice Marshall produced two special clocks in 1859. These were said to be among the finest ever made in

America and were priced at four times the cost of Van Riper's standard models. One clock was sold to the City of Nashville. The other remained in the factory warehouse after Van Riper's untimely death in 1859 and Stone and Marshall took over the business.

Cazenovia's first tower clock had been an iron one built by Jehiel Clark, Sr., and placed in the tower of the Presbyterian Church. Later it was moved to the Methodist "Old Stone Church," built in 1832. In 1862 our community's leaders replaced the old iron clock with the much-improved special Van Riper model that was in the Stone and Marshall warehouse. This valuable and historic tower clock was transferred to the taller tower/spire of the new Methodist Church (known as "The Yellow Brick Church") in January 1874. Though located in the Methodist Church, the clock was village property and considered a valuable community asset.

Trustees of the Methodist Church had tried to obtain three thousand dollars from the Cazenovia village trustees to offset the extra cost of building a tower suitable for the clock, but failed to do so. In exasperation, no doubt, the Methodist leaders passed a resolution on December 10, 1873, allowing placement of the village clock without compensation. Maintenance costs, however, still fell to the village. It appears from the historical record that the village did eventually contribute five hundred dollars to help defray the expense of installing the clock. The village budget occasionally provided a small amount of money to individuals to wind the clock in the ensuing decades, but no regular funds were expended to keep the clock in good working order.

In 1969, the Village of Cazenovia turned over maintenance of the clock to the Methodists, though the Village retained ownership of the clock. Unfortunately, keeping the clock functional became a financial burden for the congregation. Restoration and re-dedication of clock took place in 1979. Volunteers, such as Millie and Chuck Grime, members of the church, helped in the effort. Tower clock experts, most notably Russ Oechsle of Homer, Bob Caterfeld of Homer, and Bob Betz of Earlville, worked on repairing the historic clock mechanism.

Winding the clock once a week is itself a task that requires both dedication and strength. In recent years, Bob Arnold and Tom Sigle have risen to the challenge, earning them our gratitude and our admiration. The clock weights, wooden boxes filled with stone rubble, have heft to them.

The spires that once graced Cazenovia's Methodist church are long gone. They disappeared in 1953. Local lore has it that they were taken down amidst concern that they were swaying in the wind and therefore a danger to all. I have been told that this concern was probably misplaced as the spires were designed to yield some to strong gusts, just as modern skyscrapers do. In any case, they are gone, a great loss to the visual beauty of the village and to the architectural legacy of Archimedes Russell.

It would also be a matter of great pride to all members of the United Methodist Church of Cazenovia (our official name today) to once again hear the church bell rung on a regular basis. The bell, housed in the taller of the two existing towers, is the one that was transferred from the "Old Stone Church" to the "Yellow Brick Church" in 1872. It was cast in 1839 by the firm of Meneely & Oothout of West Troy (now Watervliet), New York, and can be tolled by the use of a rope or made to ring when the tower clock striker is in use. Tower or town clocks manufactured in Cazenovia are today prized for their historical significance as well as for their ingenious design and beauty. As with so much else, the manufacture of tower clocks passed from the hands of members of the guild to factory workers, such as those employed by the Seth Thomas and Howard clock-making companies. The forty-five-year long legacy of Cazenovia tower clocks came to an end with the demise of the firm of Stone, Marshall & Card in the mid-1870s. Marshall and Card were making slings for clay pigeons (used in target shooting) in their old factory in 1879.

VI. Secrets of the Cornerstone Box Revealed

"What's in the box?" The curious raise this question whenever there is talk of a cornerstone box. The first use of a cornerstone box to seal and preserve artifacts deeming historically important is, as far as I can determine, lost to history, ironic as that may seem. But the use of cornerstone boxes by religious and civic organizations has been widespread in the United States as it was in Europe. Generally, the box is not opened until the structure containing it is demolished and replaced by a newer one.

Opening a cornerstone box is like opening a time capsule. The items placed in the box are meant to signify to future generations what the people responsible for the contents deemed important. Sometimes the opening ritual can be disappointing as it was in Spartanburg, South Carolina, in 1959 when the lid was lifted off a metal box that had been mortar-sealed and placed in the county courthouse that was built in 1891. Rumors had it that the box would contain a bottle of good rye whiskey. No rye whiskey was found, though there was an old brown bound Bible.

The cornerstone box of Cazenovia's First Methodist Church is yet to be retrieved and opened. However, I can reveal the contents as reported by The Cazenovia Republican in a lead article published November 19,1933, in conjunction with the one hundredth anniversary celebration of the building of the "Old Stone Church." The laying of the cornerstone and placement of the copper box had taken place on a hot July 4, 1872, with a large crowd in attendance.

According to the newspaper's accounting, here is a list of the contents: a Bible; a Hymn Book; the Book of Discipline of the Methodist Church; a Catalogue of the Central New York Conference; the Methodist Almanac for 1872; and one copy each of the following periodicals--Christian Advocate, Northern Christian Advocate, Heathen Women's Friend, Cazenovia Republican, Sunday School Advocate, Missionary Advocate, Methodist Quarterly Review, Report of the Church Extension Society, Catalogue of Syracuse University, Ladies' Repository, Central New York Conference Minutes, and a file of the Daily Christian Advocate published during the General Conference of 1872. Note the absence of any bottle of rye whiskey. These were Methodists, good temperance folk.

With the exception of the copy of <u>The Cazenovia Republican</u> and perhaps that Syracuse University catalogue, the box's contents may not be of much significance to readers of this essay other than historians such as myself or Methodists of long standing. But taken collectively, the articles in the box tell us something significant about the people responsible for building the historic landmark that is today's Cazenovia United Methodist Church. These were Christians, of course, but demonstratively of the Methodist kind, that is to say, heirs of the Protestant ecclesiastical and spiritual tradition emanating out of England and inspired by John Wesley (1703-1791).

Born in 1703 in an Anglican rectory, John followed in the footsteps of his father Samuel by becoming a clergyman of the Church of England. However, he longed for a more earnest and deeply personal expression of Christianity than available in the formalistic and high liturgical Anglican churches of the 18th-century. Along with brother Charles and other equally pious students at the University of Oxford, John Wesley organized a "Holy Club" whose members practiced a disciplined life of prayer, Bible study, and social ministry on behalf of the poor and needy. Their methodical or disciplined approach to personal piety gave rise to the moniker "Methodist," though they did not intend to break away from the Church of England.

One of the Oxford Methodists, a traveling evangelist and dynamic preacher by the name of George Whitefield (1714-1770), carried the Methodist banner to America on seven visits. American Methodists organized themselves into a denomination of their own at the famous Christmas Conference held in Baltimore in 1784. They did so after failing to convince the bishops in England to ordain sufficient ministers for the growing numbers of Methodists in the United States. Adopting much of John Wesley's theology, his liturgy, and his hymns, American Methodism expanded rapidly during the post-Revolutionary War decades and into the first half of the 19th-century. Methodist preachers, especially those practicing an itinerant ministry with saddlebag and horse on the frontier, carried the scripture and holiness across the land.

Historians of American religion have marveled at Methodism's extraordinary popular appeal in the formative years of our nation. Methodists favored enthusiastic revivals and missionary preaching. Their appeal found fertile soil among classes of Americans whose spiritual care was being neglected by the more established denominations--especially the poor, women, and blacks. Methodism also found favor among people who wanted a distinctive American expression of religion, a faith tradition for the new republic.

When Methodists placed the cornerstone box in Cazenovia's "Yellow Brick Church" in 1872, they no longer represented a frontier denomination. Some might say that something of the missionary revival style of the earlier days had given way to a more corporate and formalistic church. However, if we look closely at what was placed in that box, we are reminded of the roots of Methodism and can, I would argue, conclude that the Methodists of 1872 treasured their heritage, no matter the passing of time since Wesley's day.

In our next, and final, installment in this series "Moments in Methodism," we shall offer a few observations about a time when the present day "Yellow Brick Church" almost ceased to be and something also of the present life of the church.

VII. Within These Walls

In this, the final installment of the "Moments in Methodism" series, I wish to offer a few reflections of the history of Cazenovia's United Methodist Church in recent memory. Historians, such as myself, must tread lightly in writing of times not long ago. Perspective, not to mention objectivity, can be distorted by the passions of the present. Having joined the Methodist congregation in Cazenovia only recently as an associate member (keeping my Lutheran identity), I do not have the long memory of some who have faithfully attended services in "The Yellow Brick Church" for decades.

John Burlew, husband of the Rev. Betty Burlew, a much beloved former pastor of the Methodists in Cazenovia (as well as those in Nelson), once corrected me by saying that I should refer to the congregation in our village as the Cazenovia **United** Methodist Church. He stressed the word **United** because of the merger in 1968 at a convention in Dallas with the Evangelical United Brethren Church. This ecclesiastical body was itself the result of a merging of two faith traditions in 1948. In that year the United Brethren Church, founded by William Otterbein and Martin Boehm among German speaking immigrants who settled mostly in rural Pennsylvania, and the Evangelical Association, led by Jacob Albright, another immigrant who pastored fellow Germans in rural Pennsylvania, joined forces. All of this may seem to some contemporary readers as a version of "the relatives" game, trivia to outsiders but vital to family members who want to know who is related to whom. As a historian of the complicated story of how Americans have created the religious landscape of today, I find this DNA sleuthing of present-day ecclesiastical communities fascinating.

Our account of the history of Cazenovia's United Methodist Church becomes even more convoluted (in a good way, I think) because our village's Methodists have from time to time been yoked with Methodist churches elsewhere in a multi-point parish. The Methodist congregations in Cazenovia, Nelson, and Erieville were at one time in partnership. Presently, the congregations in Cazenovia and Nelson belong to a single parish, sharing pastoral leadership. The multi-point parish is not unlike the form of ministry conducted by the Methodist circuit-riding preachers of days gone by. There may be much rushing about for the preacher on a Sunday morning, but there are benefits too. The Nelson Methodists famously carry on a tradition of serving tasty roast beef dinners. We in Cazenovia have our barbecue chicken extravaganzas. Apart from these culinary delights, there are mutually spiritually refreshing activities.

Given these signs of ongoing Christian life, it may come as a surprise to some readers to learn that there was a day when "The Yellow Brick Church" of Cazenovia almost ceased to be. An article in the November 8, 1989, issue of The Cazenovia Republican carried the ominous title "Church's Fate Unknown." According to the newspaper account, Cazenovia Methodists at that time voted to build a new church, though no location had been decided upon and no cost of a new building had been determined. All of this came after much discussion of the congregation's needs and a demographic survey. Some members wanted to remain in the church built in 1872, but an estimate of $800,000 had come in for repairing the brick exterior. Others argued that it would cost only $40,000 to tear down the church (excluding the cost of removing the stained glass windows, the church bell, and the tower clock).

I was not attending Cazenovia's Methodist Church in 1989 and cannot speak to the passions of the moment. I am not sure how I would have voted had I been a member, given the difficulty of balancing the economics of the situation with my respect for historic structures and tradition. The vote to build a new church was later overturned and Cazenovia Methodists still worship in "The Yellow Brick Church." Housed as we are in a large structure that is aging and in need of constant repair such as the expensive reroofing project this summer, the congregation struggles yet between the poles of economic survival and good stewardship of a beautiful building that is part of Cazenovia's Historic District.

Change is a constant of life, individually and institutionally. Perhaps you have noticed the new and amended signage beckoning one and all to enter the doors of "The Yellow Brick Church," now over 140 years old. Cazenovia Methodists and our parish partners at the Nelson church now have new ministerial leadership. The Rev. Ray Lange, an ordained Methodist elder of long experience, has assumed ministerial duties among us. Kevin McAllister, a candidate for ministry, will be sharing parish responsibilities. For more information on what is happening within the yellow brick walls of Cazenovia's historic Methodist church, see the church website: www.caznovianelsonumchurch.org

Those of you who have been watching the re-roofing project this summer, may have noticed something else. A signboard bears witness to the presence of the Summit Baptist Church within the walls of "The Yellow Brick Church." This congregation, affiliated with the Southern Baptist denomination, needed a place to worship and Cazenovia Methodists opened the doors of their historic building to Summit's leadership and members. As of this writing (December 2013), I know of no other arrangement similar to this in the Village of Cazenovia, past or present.

This welcoming attitude reminds me of something written by the Rev. Silas E. Persons in 1908. At that time Persons occupied the Presbyterian Manse in Cazenovia and had written a booklet with the title: Historical Sketch of the Religious Denominations of Madison County, 1796-1906. Persons drew attention to the squabble in 1816 when Baptists and Methodists were holding services at the "Old Court House" on alternate Sundays. It so happened that the Baptists refused to yield the space to the Methodists on a Sunday when the Methodist quarterly meeting was to be held, forcing the Methodists to assemble in an abandoned distillery. In recompense, the Methodists outbid the Baptists for the "Old Court House" when it came up for sale and the Madison County seat was moved to Morrisville. Presbyterian parson Persons editorialized in 1908: "Since then we have learned not to snub the Methodists; for the Methodists have grown, --and so has Christian courtesy."

Ministers of the Church

Fitch Reed	1825 - 1827	Lyman Sperry	1845 - 1846
John Dempster	1827 - 1829	A. J. Crandall	1846 - 1848
Zachariah Paddock	1829 - 1831	David Holmes	1848 - 1850
George Peck	1831 - 1833	D. W. Bristol	1850 - 1852
Joseph Castle	1833 - 1835	Charles D. Burritt	1852 - 1854
Nelson Rounds	1835 - 1836	William Reddy	1854 - 1856
Luke Hitchcock	1836 - 1837	Daniel A. Whedon	1856 - 1858
Vincent M. Coryell	1837 - 1838	Lyman A. Eddy	1858 - 1860
W. V. Pearne	1838 - 1840	Ephraim Hoag	1860 - 1862
Joseph Cross	1840 - 1842	Luke C. Queal	1862 - 1864
Silas Comfort	1842 - 1843	A. S. Graves	1864 - 1865
Selah Stocking	1843 - 1845		

appointed President of Cazenovia Seminary
before conclusion of year and Rev. Blain
was supply pastor.

Benjamin Shove	1865 - 1867
O. H. Warren	1867 - 1869
A. L. York	1869 - 1871
F. H. Stanton	1871 - 1873
O. L. Gibson	1873 - 1876
James Erwin	1876 - 1879
Theron Green	1879 - 1882
Charles H. Wright	1882 - 1885
Charles Eddy	1885 - 1887
Curtis N. Mogg	1887 - 1890
Frederick T. Keeney	1890 - 1893
C. M. Eddy	1893 - 1897
Theron R. Green	1897 - 1899 (Second term)
Arthur Copeland	1899 - 1900
A. W. Broadway	1900 - 1903
E. J. Rosengrant	1903 - 1904
David Keppel	1904 - 1909
Lyford S. Boyd	1909 - 1916
A. E. Hall	1916 - 1918
R. DeWitt Stanley	1918 - 1924
William W. Lane	1924 - 1927
Arthur E. Morey	1927 - 1933
Jesse Mullette	1933 - 1934
Paul F. Eberly	1934 - 1936
Ellis E. Pierce	1936 - 1939
Clytus Mowry	1939 - 1941
Leland Barnes	1941 - 1943
James W. McConnell	1943 - 1947
R. Bertrand Brett	1947 -

Source: Roberta Loyster Hendrix, <u>We Methodists: A History, Cazenovia Methodist Church, 1830-1966</u> (p. 43).

Ministers of the Cazenovia Methodist Church, cont.

R. Bertrand Brett 1947-1968

John Love 1968-1973

Henry D. Austin 1973-1984

Donald Rush 1984-1988

Frank Hale, Jr. 1988-1990

Robert Wollaber 1990-1993

Gary Hakes 1993-1995

Timothy O'Conner-Shaler 1993-1995

Neale G. Bachman 1995-1997

Keith Haverkamp 1997-1998

Robert Varnum 1998-2000

Mardean Moyer 1995-2000

Elizabeth J. Burlew 2000-2012

Robin Blair 2012-2013

Raymond Lange 2013-2015

Kevin McAllister 2015-

Cazenovia Methodist Chronology

First Methodist class in Cazenovia	1816
Madison County Courthouse purchased for church	1817
Courthouse building conveyed to conference	1823
ME Church in Cazenovia constitute as part of Genesee Conference	1825
First pastor appointed	1825
First recorded meeting of the Trustees	Nov. 19, 1830
Stone church built and dedicated	1832
First parsonage acquired	1849
Demolition of stone church	1872
Present church construction on same site	1872
Church dedication	Dec. 17, 1873
Declared debt free	1883
Parsonage on Nickerson Street acquired	1887
Renovation of church and parsonage	1900
Complete renovation and alteration of church	1924
Centennial Celebration	1933
Restoration project	1953-54
Operation "Face-Lift" Redecoration and Sandblasting	1963-1964
Replacement of Roof	1964
Church rededication	June 13, 1965
Re-pointing of brick walls and renovation of trim	Summer 1990
Replacement of Roof	1992
Dedication ceremony for restored clock	September 1997

Many other physical changes have taken place at Cazenovia Methodist since 1997. One thinks of the sale of the parsonage on Ten Eyck Avenue, improvements to the restrooms, new more energy efficient windows on the bottom level, and a major kitchen renovation. Instead of listing all of these changes, perhaps it would be of interest to focus on examples of service, mission, and ministry.

Some of these activities are parish-wide, involving members from the Cazenovia and the Nelson congregations.

Regular worship services
Sunday School
Bible Study
Choir and special music from time to time
Preparation and serving of meals at the Samaritan Center, Syracuse
Contributions to CazCares
Chicken barbecues to enable young people to attend Casowasco Camp
Chicken barbecues at Super Bowl time
Prison ministry teams
Caroling at Christmas for shut-ins
Quilting and sewing groups
Use of church space by community groups
Pie walk during the Christmas holiday period
Yard and rummage sales to raise money for the church's general fund
Monthly book club
Visitation of shut-ins

Sanctuary after Church Redication on June 13, 1965

Notes

Here is a place where you can add your own notes and reflections on the Cazenovia church.

Section II: Nelson United Methodist Church

Photos courtesy of Pastor Kevin McAllister

FIRST METHODIST EPISCOPAL SOCIETY
OF NELSON

In preparing a sketch of the First Methodist Episcopal Society of Nelson, we find ourselves handicapped at the commencement by the fact that the Quarterly Conference records prior to the year 1853 cannot be found. However by access to Conference minutes and the other books of records in possession of the Central New York Conference Historical Society at Syracuse, and the Trustee records of our own society since 1833, together with complete records since 1853, we believe that we have been able to make a practically true historical record of the society; with very few errors at least.

The earliest Methodist preaching in this vicinity was by preachers from Cazenovia. Zachariah Paddock, George Hare, Ward White and others held occasional service in private dwellings and schoolhouses. The first regular services were held in the schoolhouse near Marlin Lyon's, then known as the Hutchinson District. Among the original members of this class were Leroy Hutchinson and wife, P. Doolittle and wife, and Isaac Doolittle and wife. This class was formed sometime prior to 1930.

The class at Nelson was formed it is thought, by Rev. Seager, then pastor at Cazenovia, (but who, I think, must have been either a supply or an assistant) at about the same time. At that time, 1830, Nelson formed a part of the Lenox Circuit, which included Canastota, Clockville, Perryville, Mile Strip and Chittenango Falls, or it was connected with Cazenovia as an out appointment. It was a part of the Lenox Circuit, or was connected with Cazenovia from 1830 to 1838. Nelson was then made a separate appointment and continued so until 1845. In 1845 Nelson was again put on the Lenox Circuit and remained a part of said circuit from 1845 to 1853. In 1853 it was again constituted a separate charge with Chittenango Falls as an out appointment, and continued such from 1853 to 1865. In 1865 Chittenango Falls was taken away and Erieville became a part of the charge, and it was known as the Nelson and Erieville charge. It has continued in this relation from 1865 to the present time except the years 1869 - 1871, 1877, 1879, 1881 and 1883 when Nelson was a station with no out appointments. The Charge is now known as the Nelson and Erieville Charge, with preaching at Nelson in the morning and

Erieville afternoons and alternate Sunday evenings.

The first service held by Methodist Episcopal preachers in the village of Nelson were held in the house of Nehemiah Smith, now owned by Wallace Abbott, situated on the north side of Main Street just west of the four corners, and after a time in the schoolhouse. Among the original members of this class at Nelson were Nehemiah Smith, A.S. Hyatt, Abijah Hyatt, Allen Smith and Isaac Pierson. This class soon became the central point because of its location, and in 1833 a church organization was formed including several classes in the vicinity.

The meeting called by legal notice, for the purpose of perfecting the organization and to give it a corporate existence, was held in the home of Nehemiah Smith, on the twenty-fifth day of January 1833. Abijah Hyatt and Nehemiah Smith were chosen to preside at said meeting, and the following trustees were duly and legally elected: for the term of one year, Abijah Hyatt and William W. Clough; for two years, Ethan Allen and James Anderson; for three years, Nehemiah Smith, Jeremiah Sayles and Abel S. Pierson. It was voted "that the said Society shall be known and distinguished by the name and style of the First Society of the Methodist Episcopal Church in Nelson." The foregoing forms a complete history of the corporate existence of our society.

In 1833, Nehemiah Smith and his wife, Rhoda Smith, deeded to the First Methodist Society of the Methodist Episcopal Church in Nelson a tract of land thirty-two by fifty feet, upon which a Methodist chapel had been built during the summer. The deed is dated October 24, 1833 and was recorded on the first day of November, 1834, at 10 o'clock A.M., in Liber K of Deeds, page 20.

The society continued to use this chapel until April 1853, when because of the need of better accomodations, they purchased the Congregational church, situated on the north side of Main Street, east of the four corners, on the same lot now occupied by their present house of worship. A subscription was at once started in order to repair and remodel the building. During the summer of 1853 the repairs were made by J.C. Smith, builder, and the church was dedicated September 29, 1853. The cost of the repairs and incidental expenses in connection therewith, together with the expenses incident to the dedication amounted to $1,334, all of which was pledged, beside a surplus of $137. But there was some shrinkage when the final accounting was made, so that a small debt remained against the society until 1859, when it was finally cancelled. Rev. Thomas Harroun was preacher in charge at the time the church was purchased and repaired.

The church as thus repaired continued to meet the needs of the society until the summer of 1877, when it was again repaired and enlarged. The basement was taken out, the building lowered, stained glass windows put in, and a session room and ladies parlor were built as an annex at the rear of the church. The expense of these extensive improvements were about $2,500. The building was formally accepted by the trustees and the building committee discharged November 7, 1877. Rev. Horatio Gates, who is still a member of our Conference, was pastor at this time. As thus repaired the chapel edifice is still doing service and is kept in excellent repair. It was well painted by F.R. Gaige during the summer of 1898. [Original manuscript contains a verbatim copy of the deed given by Nehemiah and Rhoda Smith in 1833. It has been omitted here.]

Our society has numbered among her pastors many men who have become prominent in our church councils. Most prominent among these stands Rev. Bishop John P. Newman, D.D., L.L.D. Bishop Newman preached to our society the first year of his regularly appointed work. Following is a complete list of all who have served as pastors of our church from 1830 to the present time as found by consulting the official minutes of the annual conference and our own church records:

Zachariah Paddock, 1839
George Beck, 1831-32
Joseph Castle, 1833-34
N. Rounds, 1835
Luke Hitchcock, 1836
Vincent M. Coryell, 1837
Goodwin Stoddard, 1830
Alvin Torrey, 1830
Roswell Parker, 1831
Benjamin Paddock, 1832
John Watson, 1832
Eben L. North, 1833
James Atwell, 1834-35
Zetto Barns, 1834

B. G. Paddock, 1835-36
James Kelsey, 1837
Darius Anthony, 1837
Walter Hare, 1838
E. L. Wadsworth, 1839-40
John Young, 1841
L. K. Redington, 1842
Zetto Barns, 1843-44
E. C. Brown, 1845
George Colgrove, 1845
Leonard Bowdish, 1846
Oliver Hessler, 1846-47
Wesley Fox, 1848-49
John P. Newman, 1849

Lewis Anderson, 1850-51

L. H. Hartsongh, 1851

T. B. Rockwell, 1852

Thomas Harroun, 1852-53

Simon P. Gray, 1854-55

William R. Codd, 1856-57

R. H. Clark, 1858-59

H. C. Hall, 1860-61

Jospeh O. Gifford, 1862-63

Lyman A. Eddy, 1864

Orville N. Hinman, 1865

Isaac Harris, 1866-67

Francis W. Tooke, 1868-69

Lyman A. Eddy, 1870-71

Wm. E. York, 1872

John M. Brell, 1873

Charles L. F. Howe, 1874-75

Horatio Gates [or Yates], 1876-77

F. H. Stanton, 1878-79

Oren Switzer, 1880-81

Sidney A. Luce, 1882-83

Walter Statham, 1884-85

Henry Meeker, 1886-87

Hiram H. Williams, 1888-90

Howard L. Rixon, 1891-93

William G. Reed, 1894-96

Arthur W. Battey, 1897-1900

George E. Rosenberry, 1901

E. H. King, 1902

Rev. Beadle, 1903

G.W. Moxcey, 1904-05

Nelson was without a parsonage until 1856, when the house now owned by John Knox, situated on the south side of Main Street, was purchased and continued to be used as a parsonage until 1886. In 1886 an exchange was made with Mr. Meredith for the excellent and commodious two storey square house, on the south side of Main Street near the west end of the Village. This property makes one of the most pleasant parsonage properties in Cazenovia District.

Mrs. Frank Keith
Nelson, NY

G. A. Stott, 1906-1908
E. A. Peck, 1908-1910
L. F. Kelsey, 1910-1914
C. S. Dopp, 1914-1916
J. A. Gardner, 1916-1919
John P. Klotzbach, 1920-1922
Orson M. Case, 1922-1923
Ernest Devine, 1923-1926
Leon Northup, 1926-1928
Howard F. Buies, 1928-1932
E. Richard Barnes, 1932-1936
J. Wayne Hunter, 1936-1940
Ernest Butterfield, 1940-1945
Floyd De Flyer 1946-1947
Rudolf Grossman,1947-1948
Sydney Pudney, 1948-1955
L. Edmund Van Order, 1955-1962
William Bailey, 1963-1964
M. Edward Lincoln, 1964-1967
Robert De Walt, 1967-1969
Raymond L. Hill, 1969-1973
Robert J. Knapp, 1973-1981
Jerald F. Lipsius, 1981-1990
Richard Vogel, 1990-1993
Gary Hakes, 1993-1995
Neale Bachman 1995-1997

Dean Moyer 1995-2000
Keith Haverkamp 1997-1998
Robert Varnam 1998-2000
Elizabeth Burlew 2000-2012
Bruce Barden 2001-2003
Robin Blair 2012
Ray Lange 2013-2015
Kevin McAllister 2013-present

Nelson Methodist Church Chronology
Contributed by Fay Lyon

Late 1820s - Earliest Methodist preaching in this vicinity was held private dwellings and schoolhouses. The first regular services were held in a schoolhouse near Marlin Lyon's in the Town of Fenner

1830 - First services of the Methodist Episcopal Church Society were held at the home of Nehemiah Smith. A Rev. Seager, Pastor at Cazenovia, probably was the appointed pastor in Nelson and part of the Lenox Circuit

1833 - Nehemiah Smith and wife Rhoda deeded land to the society to build a Chapel thereon. The same year the society was incorporated as the "First Society of the Methodist Episcopal Church of Nelson. The chapel stood 3 buildings west of Nelson Rd on RT.20

1853 - The Trustees of the Methodist Episcopal Church purchases the old Meeting House from the Congregationalist. Members of the society receive a donation of pews from the former occupants. Joseph C Smith was contracted to repair their new purchase for the sum of $1050. He covered up the sluice in front of the church with planking, the basement was dug out for two classrooms and a conference room, the pulpit was reversed from front to rear and the galleries were removed from the sides and fitted the same up front. The pews were turned to face the pulpit where an alter was built. Other general improvements were done.
 - Their newly revamped Church was dedicated
 -Their old Chapel was sold for $250

1856 - The John Knox house(Harold & Fay Davies house), in Nelson, was purchased for a parsonage to be exchanged for the Sidney Meredith house in 1866(the Mill's place)

1865 - After years of belonging to various charges including as an appointment with Cazenovia, the Lenox Circuit, the Chittenango district and at times on its own it became associated with Erieville and became the Nelson/Erieville Charge

1877 - Major improvements were made to the church building. The basement was taken out with the building being lowered. The structure was resided and new stained glass windows were installed. A new session room was added to the rear of the edifice and a second floor level was designated as the "Ladies Parlor" and to grace it all a new towering steeple was added to the structure.
The expense of the new improvements totaled $2900 and they were dedicated in the fall of 1877

1913 - The parsonage was moved to Erieville and the Charge became the Erieville/Nelson Charge

1955 - The basement was dug out again and a kitchen and dining room were constructed along with new bathrooms.

1964 - A new parsonage was built next to the Nelson Church and the Charge reverted back to Nelson/Erieville

1968 - Nelson Methodist becomes Nelson United Methodist as it unites with Evangelical United Brethren Church

1983 - Nelson United Methodist celebrates sesquicentennial

1993 - Nelson Church becomes part of Cazenovia/ Erieville/Nelson Parish (CEN)

2003 - Caz/Nelson continues as Erieville leaves Parish

2009 - Nelson United Methodist sells its parsonage

2010 - Nelson United Methodist buys land to provide for more parking and drills a new well

Notes

Here is a place where you can add your own notes and reflections on the Nelson church.

REFLECTIONS
by
Dr. Milton C. Sernett

The section is made up of essays that I wrote on a monthly basis and distributed at worship services at the Cazenovia United Methodist Church and the Nelson United Methodist Church. I began doing so in October 2011.

October 2011

Thoughts for Reformation Sunday

Though worshipping with Methodists today, I confess to having German Lutheran roots. I was baptized and confirmed at Trinity Lutheran Church in Hampton, Iowa. I graduated from Concordia Lutheran Seminary, St. Louis in 1968, and I taught 3 years at Concordia Theological Seminary, Springfield, Illinois before joining the faculty of Syracuse University in 1975.

When a Fulbright scholar in Germany at the Kennedy Institute, Free University, Berlin, I made a pilgrimage down to Wittenberg and stood over the grave of Martin Luther in All Saints' Church, commonly known as the Castle Church or *Schlosskirche*. I marveled at the famous door where on Oct. 31, 1517 Luther (then a Roman Catholic priest) nailed a copy of his 95 theses (in Latin) protesting, among other things, the Pope's practice of selling indulgences to raise money. Luther's actions helped spark the Protestant Reformation.

In the days of my youth back in Iowa, we heard sermons by Pastor Linder from the pulpit of Trinity each Reformation Sunday that in essence gave me the impression that I should be thankful that I was a Lutheran and not a member of the local Roman Catholic Church--where doctrinal error such as the belief in Purgatory abounded, folks had to obey the Pope, and eat fish on Fridays. There was an irony in all of this. My father had a Czech or Bohemian background and Roman Catholic upbringing. His marriage to my German

Lutheran mother was then called a "mixed marriage" and he converted to Lutheranism.

Flash forward some 60 or more years. Now I am attending a Methodist church in Cazenovia, New York. Now it is a fact that there are no Lutheran churches in all of Madison County today--never have been, but plenty of Methodist congregations. So how do I make a spiritual connection between my Lutheran roots and my present circumstances?

Thankfully, John Wesley did it for me, or one might better say, the Holy Spirit did it for Wesley some 221 years after Luther nailed his 95 theses to the door of the Castle Church in Wittenberg. Wesley's journal entry for May 24, 1738, describes his Aldersgate Experience. Recently returned from an unsuccessful missionary trip to the American Colonies, Wesley was in low sprits. But upon hearing the Moravian preacher that night expound on Martin Luther's commentary on the St. Paul's Letter to the Romans, Wesley felt that his "heart was strangely warmed."

At last Wesley understood the full significance of Luther's emphasis upon "justification by faith alone." The hallmark doctrine of the Protestant Reformation took hold of Wesley and ignited a spiritual energy in him that had monumental consequences for the Methodist revival that followed.

My "heart was strangely warmed" on Christmas Day in 1996. My heart decided to throw a tantrum and I ended up in the cardiac unit of St. Joseph's Hospital. I wrote about that experience in an essay published in the newsletter of Faith Lutheran Church, Cicero, New York--where my wife Jan and I worshipped for more than thirty years. From 1979 to 2007, I wrote a monthly "Reflections Column" for our church newsletter, some 260 of them. I published these essays in a book of about four hundred pages in 2007 and named the book "Heart Strangely Warmed" not knowing that I would someday be among Methodists with the theological legacies of both Martin Luther and John Wesley intertwined.

Now I can celebrate Reformation Sunday in October and Aldersgate Day in May.

November 2011

On the Art of Giving Thanks

"I'm the Amen-er!" shouts the 3-year old, to which his sister quickly responds, "And I'm the pray-er." With luck, they get the timing right and our family meals proceed with only the usual confusion. More often than not, the Amen-er jumps the gun, throwing older sister off stride and causing a small in-house ecumenical disaster. As a counter measure, the six-year-old has taken to speed praying, reciting her "God is great, God is good, and we thank Him for our food" at a clip that not even her maternal grandfather, a real champion pray-er, could have matched.

Recently, no doubt in exasperation, the youngest announced that he was not going to pray at all. "Why?" I asked him. "Because it's not hot," he replied. True, we were having cold sandwiches, but such a straightforward response left me dumbfounded and caused me to reflect on some pray-ers I have known.

I recall that my Aunt Martha counseled that you only had to pray if you had more than three things. Apparently, this ruled out having to give thanks for the incidental cookie and glass of milk or piece of candy, consumed in serial fashion with sufficient interludes. A well-meaning Sunday school teacher once instructed her charges that children who loved Jesus should be able to pray at any time and under any circumstances, even when cooling parched throats at the school drinking fountain. After trial and error, I concluded that she simply did not know the idiosyncrasies of school water fountains. Unless you approached them with respect and total concentration, they returned the favor with a hard shot to the eyes and nose. Praying and drinking, I concluded, are as incompatible as simultaneously riding a two-wheeler and practicing a Beethoven sonata.

My fondest recollections about pray-ers come from many Iowa summers spent on Uncle Charlie's farm. It was his custom to conclude breakfast with a daily reading of the Scriptures as assigned by Portals of Prayer. When "Pa" turned to get his reading glasses and hand-worn King James Bible off the kitchen shelf, seven boys (a visiting cousin or two included) and "Ma" settled back for devotions. In a reverent monotone made interesting because German had been the tongue of his youth, Uncle Charlie read the Biblical text, always approaching those multi-syllabic unpronounceable Old Testament names, like Mephibosheth and Mesopotamia, with the same caution and respect he gave the Hereford bull. Not until "Pa" had concluded devotions with a short, unpretentious, and farmer's-helper-practical prayer of thanks did the day officially begin.

November is a good month for hard, serious praying. The Pilgrims, as every school child knows, set aside a day for thanksgiving in the year of Our Lord 1621. With the harvest stored against the scarcity of yet another winter, the Plymouth colonists turned in gratitude toward the Creator and Sustainer of all life. Their example is worth following. Now you be the pray-er and I'll be the Amen-er!

The Christmas Cow Is Missing!

This Christmas piece was to be about the cow in the stable-room, a meditation on that verse in the "Away in a Manger" song about "lowing cattle" waking "the little Lord Jesus." One often sees a cow or two in manger scenes this time of year. But much to my surprise, I discovered that neither ox nor ass is specifically mentioned in the infancy narratives. In fact, Luke only tells us that the Christ Child was to be found "lying all wrapped up in a manger" (Luke 2: 12). The Greek word *phatann*, translated as "manger," suggests a stall or even a feeding place open to the stars. But the cow is missing! Not a single bovine is to be found in the biblical text.

What can this all mean? Could the poets, artists, Christmas card designers, makers of manger sets, and countless small children sweetly singing "Away in a Manger" all have it wrong? I thought of church sextons the world over wearily dusting off plastic-molded Christmas cows, gluing on broken legs and tails, and trucking them out for yet one more season. Front-lawn nativity sets with placid cows are everywhere among us. Should I shout, "Leave the cow behind!"? But as long as I can remember, cows have been part of Christmas.

More so than any other holiday, American Christmas preparations are filled with fact and fancy. We dreamily call to mind Christmas past and in reverie muse upon the joys of traditional family gatherings when everyone got along "just fine." Even Uncle Al behaved himself by not imbibing too much "good cheer." Christmas tugs at the heartstrings, filling adults with child-like feelings of magic and wonder. How good the old times were!

Yet psychologists tell us that during the holiday season many people fall into depression. Some even contemplate suicide. Their memories of Christmas past starkly contrast with Christmas present. Some individuals can feel lonely and forgotten at this time of year, especially if they are away from family, confined to a hospital or nursing home, or soldiering in some distant land.

In 1688 the Swiss doctor Johannes Hofer was serving among Swiss soldiers in Northern Europe. These men were so homesick that they gave evidence of physical and emotional stress. Dr. Hofer diagnosed their affliction as *Heimweh*, a word he coined to describe the effects of homesickness. Simply to play a familiar herder's tune moved the soldiers in reverie back to their alpine homes and left a deep sorrow for beloved landscapes now lost to them on the field of battle. Engaged as we are in meeting the demands of the present and the future, *Heimweh* may overcome us too. We long for the past when the Christmas cow was in her place and all was right with the World, or so we imagine.

I am not an expert on bovine character, although I can tell an Aberdeen-Angus from a Shorthorn, a Guernsey from a Holstein, and I seem to recall that our improved breeds of cattle are descended from the wild ox of Europe and Asia. For millennia, cattle and human civilization have been indissolubly linked. Hindus, as is generally known, reverence the sacred cow, protected by a taboo against eating beef. Perhaps less well known is the fact that Scandinavian Lutherans built barns before they built houses, sleeping along side their cattle throughout the long winter nights of the Upper Plains. Pioneers would rather lose a good horse than a good cow, so essential was her milk and butter to daily existence.

Walter Wangerin, Jr., has written a best-selling fanciful tale, entitled <u>The Book of the Dun Cow</u>, in which a cow becomes something of a Christ-figure and gives her life for the other creatures. If the purpose of the cow is to point to the Christ-child in the manger, to move us from Heimweh to joyous celebrations and hope for the present and future, then I say, "Keep the cow in Christmas!"

The Cattle are lowing, the Baby awakes.
But little Lord Jesus, no crying He makes.
I love Thee, Lord Jesus, look down from the sky;
And stay by my cradle till morning is nigh.

Note:

Some readers may detect a Lutheran slant in this month's Reflections. Contrary to popular belief, the German reformer Martin Luther did not write the lyrics of "Away in a Manger," even though the song is sometimes called "Luther's Cradle Hymn." The origin of the lullaby remains a mystery.

There are no Christmas sermons in the collected works of John Wesley. Because of the Puritan revolution, the celebration of the traditional English Christmas had declined in England during the 1700s when John Wesley sparked a revitalization movement within the Anglican church. Methodists itinerant preachers in America used Christmas Day in 1784 to organize themselves into an American conference at Lane Chapel in Baltimore, Maryland.

Do You Have a Storm Home for 2012?

So far this snow season we don't have much to boast of and may not win the Golden Snowball award. But Syracuse officially recorded 192.1 inches of snow in 1992-93. Since moving to the country weather facts such as these has taken on new meaning for me. The climb up Ridge Road from the lower plateau on which the city sits and the drive along the open stretch of road between Route 173 and our driveway can make for an interesting journey, snow tires or not. Neighbors tell us of winters forty years ago when the roads drifted shut after the snowplows made the late afternoon run. Sometimes people who worked in Syracuse had to abandon their cars in the worst stretch and hike home on cold winter nights. I feel sorry for Floridians who don't have lake effect to contend with or wind chills of minus 40. How can you develop moral character if you live in a place where the weatherman or weather lady has nothing more to talk about than an occasional light frost?

Garrison Keillor, America's premier storyteller, offers us a parable for the New Year that is worth pondering in the midst of winter. Children who rode the country bus into Lake Woebegone were each given a piece of paper at the beginning of the school year with the name of their storm home written on it. His was a little green cottage down by the lake that belonged to an elderly couple, Mr. and Mrs. Kruger. Whenever a blizzard prevented the school buses from making the return run, the children were to go to their storm homes in town and remain there in the care of their storm parents until the all-clear sign was given. Garrison's family was Protestant. The Kruger's were Catholic. Protestant mothers and fathers worried that the storm home plan was a ruse devised by the Pope. Little Protestant kids were to be taken in during blizzards and put in a corner to say the Rosary for their supper. Garrison placed little stock in such talk and walked by the Kruger house often, dreaming of what it would be like on a dark, wintry afternoon to knock on the door of the little green cottage and be welcomed by the Krugers as their storm child.

Blizzards, Keillor reminds us, are not the only storms in life, and not necessarily the worst thing to worry about. Thanks to insulated homes and central heating, we can always close out the worst of winter, sheltering ourselves against Mother Nature's temper tantrums. It is much more difficult to shut out the storms of life, those trials and tribulations that come our way without warning. None of us has the gift of prophecy, so we cannot anticipate what the new year will bring. Will 2012 be remembered as one filled with more joy than sorrow, or more sorrow than joy? Whatever the next twelve months bring, it would be wise for each of us to have a storm home--a place of refuge where we can go and receive an unconditional welcome. Cazenovia Methodist Church maintains an open door policy. You can't buy a membership card. You don't have to pass a qualifying exam. You will not be refused a helping hand, no matter how far you have strayed from the fold, and you don't have to say the Rosary, or anything else, for your supper.

Emily Dickinson (1830-1886) is now recognized as one of America's great poets, yet the literary world did not know of her genius until after her death. She was a "private poet" who spent her entire life in the Dickinson Homestead on Main Street in Amherst, Massachusetts. Emily kept to herself. The two thousand manuscript poems her sister found in her bureau after her death were a surprise to her family. Emily was a religious and social recluse who rarely left home. During the last quarter century of her life she cut herself off from the outside world.

Yet her poetry is rich with insight into the human condition. "Futile the winds to a heart in port," she wrote. We are left to wonder what port it was that sheltered Emily. She did not attend church, having broken with the religious orthodoxy of the day when she was twenty-four. Perhaps it was in the poetic imagination that she sought refuge from the storms raging outside her bedroom window and in her life. Emily apparently enjoyed the solitude she wrapped herself in, even demanded it. But I cannot banish the image from my mind of a lonely New England girl who, finding no storm home in the company of others, retreated into herself.

Unlike Emily, you have a storm home--the fellowship of Christian believers that gathers regularly around Word and Sacrament. Let the winds blow. You are in the company of one who can calm every fear, every anxiety. Do you recall the story of Jesus and his disciples in the little boat on the Sea of Galilee? A great storm of wind arose and the waves beat against the ship. In a great state of alarm, the disciples awoke Jesus, who had been asleep in the back of the boat, and asked Him, "Master, do you care if we perish?" Jesus, the Fourth Chapter of the Gospel of Mark tells us, "rebuked the wind and said unto the sea, Peace, be still. And the wind ceased, and there was a great calm." When discontent of soul or sadness of heart descends upon you in 2012 like a great blanket of snow and hostile winds that blow outside, then remember this. You have a storm home in Christ who rules over all and among your friends at Cazenovia United Methodist Church who honor His Name.

February 2012

Thin Ice!

Now that February has arrived, Sunday mornings bring out the ice fishermen on Oneida Lake. Ice fishing puzzles me. I have not the courage to venture onto thin ice and can only speculate as to what those ice fishermen do in their shanties when the rest of us are in church. Perhaps they gather in prayer circles, asking God to keep it cold so that they do not find themselves plunging to the bottom of a glacial lake. Actually, ice fishing works contrary to congregating for worship, since too many ice fishing enthusiasts concentrated in one place could prove dangerous to them all. So I imagine the dedicated ice fisherman sitting in solitary confinement, waiting for a strike, chilled to the bone, and cussing himself for forgetting to bring an ice spud with which to test the thickness of the foundation of his small universe.

Perhaps I am altogether wrong, and ice fishing is an enjoyable sport. I hear tell of ice anglers who enjoy all the comforts of home (shanties equipped with carpets, televisions, and portable heaters). Hypothermia is the least of their worries. Some safety conscious anglers take personal flotation devices with them in case thin ice gives way and they find themselves taking a plunge. The bolder, or fool hearty, as the case may be, drive their cars onto the frozen expanse of their favorite lake, thereby shortening the walk from supply wagon to shanty. No matter that a vehicle or two breaks through each season.

It strikes me that those die-hard ice fishermen ought to be lured into church, where it is warm and comfortable. I say this because they seem to be a forlorn lot, left out of any denomination's mission strategy. Where is the ice fisherman's chaplain? The Navy, Army, and Air Force have chaplains. Why not ice fishermen? We are sadly deficient in ministering to those sitting on thin ice. There are no Psalms for Ice Fishermen, no Hymns, no special Liturgical settings. Ice fishermen have a variety of specialized equipment—jigging lures called Berkley Power Wigglers, depth finders known as transducers, ice augers, and polypropylene socks. They are better equipped at catching walleye and pickerel than the church is in hooking them.

Perhaps those who sit staring into black holes on frozen lakes are not as devoid of Biblical literacy as I imply. According to In-Fisherman magazine, veteran anglers know of the "Judas" principle. It works like this. A hopeful angler puts one big bait in the middle of his jigging holes. The larger bait vibrates, attracting fish from greater distances than is possible with the smaller-sized bait in the surrounding holes. As the fish make their way to the larger or Judas bait (which is too big for them to eat), they encounter the smaller jigs and are caught. Their hunger for the big bait has betrayed them.

There may be a moral lesson in this, not just for anglers active in the sport of ice fishing, but for all Christians. We can be betrayed by casting all caution aside and going for the big prize—the one thing we think will be the answer to our problems. Like the novice fisherman, who contrary to all advice about the difficulties of catching a good walleye, decides to pack only his new Jigging Rapala lure, we are sometimes tempted to put our faith in technique rather than substance. There is no one answer to how best to maintain a healthy spiritual life in the midst of the tumult of daily life. Religious fads, like fishing contraptions, come and go. The latest "hot" book or religious guru with something to sell will, like those shiny lures in the fisherman's tackle box, inevitably prove disappointing.

Ice fishermen have one gadget that sounds useful to landlubbers such as myself. It is called a tip-up. It works something like this. Rather than sitting on the ice near a small hole in sub-zero weather, the fisherman places a device over the hole which tips-up, displaying a flag or in some other fashion signaling that a fish has been caught. This way the fisherman can sit by the fire on shore or, as they do in Wisconsin (so my brother tells me), take comfort with friends in a nearby tavern. If tip-ups were equipped with radio signals, they could even alert fishermen attending church.

Unfortunately, there is no spiritual equivalent of the ice fisherman's tip-up. I know of no shortcut by which Christians can win the prize and avoid the pain. The journey of faith involves risk. As long as we are part of this mortal coil, we skate on thin ice. As with winter walkers on ice-covered water, we do well to take caution and follow the basic guidelines for survival in event we should fall into spiritual depths over our heads. Fortunately, God provides a safety net. God, in Jesus Christ, has already seen our falling through and come to the rescue. Amazing Grace!

An Angler's Prayer
> *I pray that I may fish until my dying day,*
> *and, when it comes to my last cast;*
> *I then most humbly pray,*
> *when in the Lord's great landing net*
> *and peacefully asleep;*
> *that in His mercy I be judged*
> *big enough to keep.*

Looking for a Good Woman?

The month of March has been dedicated as "Women's History" month. Over in Seneca Falls at the National Women's Hall of Fame one can find much to celebrate. The Seneca Falls story begins in 1848 when Elizabeth Cady Stanton, Lucretia Mott and some three hundred women and a few men (including Frederick Douglass) gathered to promote the rights of women, including the right to vote. They met at Seneca Fall's Wesleyan Methodist Church, whose abolition-minded members also favored the equality and rights of women. The first Women's Rights Convention issued a Declaration of Sentiments, modeled after this country's Declaration of Independence. It read, in part:

We hold these truths to be self-evident: that all men and women are created equal; that they are endowed by their creator with certain inalienable rights; among these are life, liberty, and the pursuit of happiness; that to secure these rights governments are instituted, deriving their just powers from the consent of the governed.

These words did not become self-evident in the law until 1920 and the passage of the 19th amendment giving women the right to vote. It had been a long and hard fight. Stanton did not live to see the culmination of the crusade that she helped spark in her hometown of Seneca Falls, New York. She died in 1902. Elizabeth's father had said upon the occasion of his only son's death when Elizabeth was quite young, "Oh, my daughter, I wish you were a boy." Much of her life was dedicated to proving him wrong.

Hundreds of women have been honored by being inducted into the National Women's Hall of Fame since it opened in 1969. Stanton was highly critical of the organized churches of her day. As a youngster, she heard the great revivalist Charles G. Finney preach and was both frightened and later appalled by his vivid descriptions of the torments of the unrepentant in hell. As a women's rights crusader, she faulted the orthodox Christian churches for their failure to take up the flag of reform on behalf of women everywhere.

Knowing this, I was curious to see how prominent a place "women of faith" have in the Hall of Fame at Seneca Falls.

I was pleased to discover, among others, such notables as Mother Cabrini (Maria Frances Cabrini), known as the "patron saint to immigrants." Pope Pius XII canonized her in 1946, the first American to be so honored. Then there is Mary Baker Eddy of the Christian Scientists, hailed as "the only American woman to found a lasting American-based religion." Mrs. Eddy died in 1910. Betty Bone Schiess, inducted in 1994, is honored for her efforts to open up the Episcopal Church in America to the ordination of women. I also found Bishop Leontine Kelly, who in 1984 became the first African American woman elected to the office of bishop in the United Methodist Church. There are more "women of faith" on the honor roll, too many to chronicle here. Still the list is far from complete. The Women's Hall of Fame has a website where you can nominate individuals for induction into the rank of notable women.

I have a few to nominate myself. Yes, of course, one thinks of astronauts like Sally Ride and accomplished scientists such as the zoologist Rachel Carson (d. 1964) who in her book Silent Spring sounded the alarm about the damaging effects of pesticides and other chemicals on the environment. I want to nominate unsung "women of faith" such as my mother Wilma Henrietta nee Berghoefer Sernett (d. 1988). She it was who took me to be baptized, sent me to Sunday School, and prayed for me as I journeyed down the road of life. I am sure that you have your own mothers of the faith who should be honored this month and every month of the year.

Speaking of good women, I recall a conversation that I had with my brother-in-law. I'm not sure now of the context, but it may have been in one of those talks we have as we are riding around the Illinois countryside in his pickup truck. Happily married to a good woman these many years, my brother-in-law wondered out loud where he would ever find another one like his wife should anything, God forbid, happen to her. Without thinking, I blurted out, "At JoAnn's Fabrics or A. C. Moore"–both stores where the distaff side of the gender equation seem to congregate. It was a joke, of course, maybe not a very good one. Nevertheless, I think that my brother-in-law got the point. His odds were better at these fabric and craft stores than say at NAPA, where they sell auto parts, mostly to males. In retrospect, I wish that I had said, "Well, you could check out your church."

The Bible has its own stories of "women of faith." Think of Deborah, Esther, Hannah, Sarah, Ruth, and Mary. I am partial to the story of Ruth for personal reasons. You remember, I hope, how Ruth left her own people out of loyalty to her mother-in-law Naomi and her God. Do you recall those moving words?

Entreat me not to leave you or to return from following you; for where you go I will go, and where you lodge I will lodge; your people shall be my people, and your God my God; where you die I will die, and there will I be buried. May the LORD do so to me and more also if even death parts me from you. Ruth 1:16-17

This turns out to have been the wedding text Pastor Killian used in 1965 when Jan and I were married.

April 2012

Come, Walk with Me!

"We have but one life. We get nothing out of that life except by putting something into it. To relieve suffering, to help the unfortunate, to do kind acts and deeds is, after all, the one sure way to secure happiness or to achieve real success. Your life and mine shall be valued not by what we take...but by what we give."-- Edgar F. Allen

Edgar Fiske Allen made a fortune in the lumber business. His company supplied all of the cedar logs for the American Telephone and Telegraph Company when it was expanding services coast-to-coast in the early part of the last century. Semi-retired and living in Elyria, Ohio, with his wife and two sons, Mr. Allen's life was irrevocably changed on May 30, 1907.

Two days earlier, he had attended a meeting where the topic of the inadequacy of the small community's medical services was discussed. Then on the 30th, Allen's son Homer was injured in a streetcar accident. Homer's legs had to be amputated; he died shortly thereafter. Had Elyria had better medical facilities, Homer's life might have been saved.

Edgar Allen grieved but he also saw his son's death as a life changing event and wrote in his journal: "I had spent up to that time all my life with the thought of two things: business success and money making, and my family. This was to be the turning point of my life." Edgar Fiske Allen sold his company and campaigned to build a modern hospital for the Elyria community. The Elyria Memorial Hospital opened on October 30, 1908. Allen took special interest in the children who came to the hospital, including a boy named Jimmy who came in with crippled legs. "Daddy" Allen now saw the need for a special facility for crippled children, and on April 15, 1915, the Gates Hospital for Crippled Children opened, the first such place of healing in the United States.

Allen subsequently got the Rotary Clubs of Ohio involved in raising funds for crippled children. The State of Ohio formed the Ohio Society for Crippled Children in 1919. In 1921, Allen was named president of the National Society for Crippled Children. By the time of Allen's death in 1937, there was an international society and an annual campaign to sell seals in order to raise funds. In 1952, the lily, a symbol of spring, was adopted as the official logo of the National Society for Crippled Children. By 1967, the Easter "seal" was so widely identified with this philanthropic effort to provide medical services to children and adults with disabilities and special needs that the organization changed its name to "Easter Seals." Now, as Paul Harvey would say, you know the rest of the story.

The Easter Seals mailing will arrive in your mailbox shortly, if it has not already shown up. Do not trash it along with the many other solicitations that show up at this time of year. Those Easter Seals offer an opportunity to join in the nation-wide effort to assist persons with disabilities and their families. The Americans with Disabilities Act (ADA), which was passed in 1990, requires that as a society we offer anyone with a mental or physical disability equal access to public facilities and full civil rights. Though this has been an important step forward, such a law cannot guarantee that the disabled have adequate material support to meet their medical and personal needs. This must continue to be a volunteer effort in the spirit of "Daddy" Allen.

When I was growing up, there was no federal legislation requiring that public buildings have ramps and doors allowing, for example, wheel chair bound Americans ready access. The disabled in our small community were dependent on others, usually family or friends, for so many everyday needs. Trinity Lutheran Church, built early in the last century, had a huge flight of steps leading up to the narthex. Our Lutheran disabled were kept out by such impediments. I am sure that we also had our share of the mentally handi-capped, but they were hidden from view, isolated at home for the most part or shunted off so some special state-run facility. There was one man who lived with his elderly mother in a small shack-like house on the west side of town. He spent most of his time riding about on his bicycle and displaying odd and erratic behavior, much to the amusement of some locals. I remember he showed up once in our adult Sunday School Class, brought to Trinity by some well-meaning soul. The man disrupted our minister's talk with gesticu-lations and off-subject but harmless remarks. Rev. Lindner was clearly irritat-ed by this. I was embarrassed–for our preacher, for our congregation, and for all of Christendom.

The Easter story celebrates the life and resurrection of the Lord Jesus, who once commanded the paralytic to, "Rise, Take Up Your Bed and Walk!" This month we have an opportunity to walk with those who suffer from disa-bilities of one kind or another.

Take that challenge. Go the extra mile.

May 2012

To the Ladies that Sew

"Hands to Work and Hearts to God"

(Shaker saying)

Mother's old Singer treadle-powered sewing machine sat in a corner in our Iowa home's sunroom, beneath a plaque that said, "A Stitch in Time Saves Nine." That machine empowered Wilma Henrietta (nee Berghoefer) Sernett. Though she patronized the stores founded by Mr. Sears and J.C. Penny, mother stretched her nurse's salary by taking 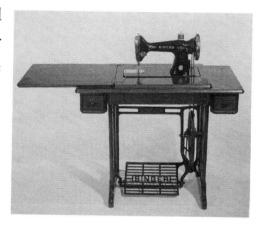 clothes donated by my older cousins and remaking them so that I did not look like a scarecrow in duds twice my size. Mother mended and patched, stitched and darned, because she wanted her four children to look decent when they went to school. Though her income was less than $375 a month in the 1950s, she was not about to have the Sernett kids called ragamuffins.

When I was alone in Germany on a Fulbright for a year in 1994-95, I missed my wife, in part because she inherited from her mother skills with needle and thread. Jan sent me off to Berlin with one of those emergency sewing kits, and I did manage to re-attach a button or two. These small repairs served to remind me of how dependent I had become on her. We will celebrate forty-seven years of marriage this year. During this time, Jan has spent countless hours at her Sears sewing machine, given to us by my mother as a wedding gift in 1965, as well as at three newer machines that are technological marvels. Jan's pattern collection rivals that at JoAnn Fabrics, a store dear to her heart, and she has created scores of wonderful garments over the years, ranging from our daughter Rebecca's baptismal outfit to a long blue dress Jan has worn on special occasions for over two decades. Then there are the more prosaic items—like the black fabric extenders on my flannel pajama sleeves. Who else but a loving wife (or mother) could a guy go to get flannel pajama extenders? I am aware that these reflections on ladies sewing violate today's gender politics, but then I still enjoy watching old Lawrence Welk shows.

Sewing was not always women's work. In the Old World, Jewish males plied treadle and bobbin in a trade that was in part inherited and in part, the result of social discrimination by dominant Christian groups. During the Victorian period in England, middle-class women were taking up painting and writing and, like their upper-class counterparts, they began to think that sewing and mending was best left to uneducated lower-class women (seamstresses) and male Jewish tailors who kept shops in the back alleys of London. English social reformers wrote of the plight of the distressed seamstress, and early feminists argued that the dull, repetitive act of plying the needle symbolized a woman's confinement to the domestic sphere. Seamstresses were "slaves of the needle."

Tell that to the ladies of our congregation (my wife included) who gather at church to sew or who are quilters and you might get an argument. When we were active members at Faith Lutheran Church, Cicero, the sewing group had a closet of material odds and ends located in the sacristy, not far from the staples of "bread and wine" used during our celebration of the Holy Sacrament. This is right, fitting, and proper, for the sewing ladies were engaged in their own ministry of reconciliation. They took ordinary scraps of cloth and pieced them into blankets in order to bring warmth and comfort to God's poor worldwide. When set against the sum total of humanity's need, the approximately several hundred quilts the ladies have made to date may not impress the skeptic, but to each of the recipients a warm blanket is a Godsend. Somewhere this very night, a child in a land far away sleeps under a quilt bearing the label "Made by the Women of Faith Lutheran Church, Cicero, New York." I know about those iron-on transfer labels. I made them myself.

Perhaps quilting is a higher art than sewing, bearing the same relationship as, for example, portraiture does to house painting. I have seen prize-winning quilts of exquisite design and clever use of color and fabric. These museum pieces rival Joseph's "amazing Technicolor" coat in their power to evoke an emotional response. You will recall how Jacob made his son Joseph "a coat of many colors" as a token of his great love. My Hebrew is rusty, so I am not sure if the original verb implies that Jacob himself stitched the garment together or if the Hebrew verb is a transitive one, signifying agency by another, such as a seamstress. In any case, this quilted coat proved to be the envy of Joseph's brothers, and they took it from him before they cast him into a pit.

Patchwork creations still evoke powerful emotions. Heirloom quilts tie the generations together, and heritage quilts preserve a community's story for our children's children. Quilts can also be small sacraments of love, testaments to the greater love that God has shown each of us. So here is a tribute to the hands and hearts of those who sew and quilt. Like the artisans who fashioned the stained glass windows of the greatest cathedrals in the world, they work to the glory of God.

May their number increase.

June 2012

"Fare Thee Well"

This month we say our goodbyes to the Rev. Elizabeth Burlew, the faithful pastor of the Cazenovia and Nelson United Methodist Churches. Ever the nurturing spiritual caregiver these past twelve years, "Pastor Betty," as our minister is known in the churches and the communities she has served, is retiring, a mixed blessing. We lose someone dear to us; she, in turn, can devote her considerable talents to other interests. Saying goodbye is always difficult, especially where strong bonds of mutual respect and affection have been fostered over time.

I hail from the Midwest--Iowa to be exact. My farm relatives struggled to express their feelings in words, too much stolid German Lutheranism in them. Yet when we drove out to Uncle Ed and Aunt Emma's place on summer evenings they took us in as if we belonged there. Mother would visit with the adults while the four of us Sernett "kids" ran around outside, harassing the chickens and playing tag in and out of the shadows of the yard light. Finally, it was time to go home. We were called into the kitchen to say goodbye, then said more goodbyes as we left and got into our car. Uncle Ed and Aunt Emma would follow us to mother's Plymouth. More talk--more goodbyes. Mother, anxious to get us home and into bed, would start her car. Still more talk, sometimes with one of the Berghoefers poking his or her head into an open window while the farm dogs jumped up on the side of our car. Finally, mother would slowly back away. We'd see our uncle and aunt standing in the twilight, waving every so warmly. Then, with darkness settling in and the stars coming out, we pulled out of the driveway--but not without two toots on the car horn. Two toots when you say goodbye--that was the unwritten rule back in Iowa.

How shall we say our goodbyes to Pastor Betty and husband John later this month? It will be, as all would agree, a double loss, for John Burlew, a veteran of the Navy, has sailed the high

seas of life with Pastor Betty these many years, been to her and to us a steady anchor of both compassion and faith. We salute him for his faithful watch service in the church fellowship and in the community at large. I am told that there is no official Navy motto. The Marines have "Semper Fi," as any devotee of the NCIS television show knows. Some claim that the Navy's motto is "Honor, Courage, Commitment." If that is the case, John Burlew embodies it. Others say it is "Non sibi sed patriae" ("Not self but country"). "Not self but Christ" may best embody what Pastor Betty and John have taught us these twelve years.

The bloggers and advice givers in this modern age are only too ready to prime the pump, telling us what to say when saying goodbye. Some quote Dale Evans: "Happy trails to you, until we meet again." Dr. Seuss said, "Don't cry because it's over. Smile because it happened." Garrison Keillor advises us to say: "Be well, do good work, and keep in touch." If you like William Shakespeare, you might want to tell Pastor Betty and John: "Farewell! God knows when we will meet again." Nicholas Sparks, author of The Notebook, wrote: "The reason it hurts so much to separate is because our souls are connected." Good ol' Charlie Brown offers this gem: "Absence makes the heart grow founder, but it sure makes the rest of you lonely."

Pastor Betty and John will appreciate whatever you say from the heart, no matter how ineloquent. Perhaps the best way to say goodbye to Pastor Betty and John is to continue the ministry of love and service that they have so faithfully modeled since coming into our midst twelve years ago.

So wish them a hearty farewell, not as in goodbye, but as in
"Fare Thee Well"!

July 2012

On Reaching the Half Century Mark-twenty years later!

Here are some reflections that I wrote in July 1992

This month yours truly celebrates his fiftieth birthday. I doubt that the event will be much noted or commented on outside of the family circle, so I beg the indulgence of 'Reflections' readers to make public a few thoughts on reaching the half-century mark. Aging is a peculiar process, as those of you who are my seniors can vouchsafe. I was not much conscious of getting older until one day some years ago when in one of those spontaneous foot races both of my children outran me. The sensation was strange--in my mind I was humming along, but apparently my legs, at least in comparison to those of Rebecca and Matthew, were going in slow motion. It was a humbling experience, especially for someone who once ran a mean final leg on the 440 meter Hampton High School relay team.

When we are young and full of dreams, growing older seems so remote a concern that we avoid serious consideration of the consequences. I have distinct memories of sitting Sunday after Sunday in the rear pew of Trinity Lutheran Church back in Iowa with my brother, two sisters, and mother. To amuse myself during Pastor Lindner's sermons, which were directed at adults and not children, I studied the nodding heads in front of us, especially those of the elderly farmers who seemed as much part of the furniture of our church as the oak pews. Among these ancients was Old John Behn, known as "Grandpa" to Curtis, my high school friend and Confirmation classmate. Though stoop shouldered and retired from the heavy fieldwork, Grandpa Behn enjoyed his octogenarian status. He had a bedroom of his own on the family farm, tended to a large garden and orchard, and cared for a small flock of sheep. When our family visited the Behn farm, we often encountered Grandpa puttering about, apparently happy with his lot in life and celebrating in his remarkably contented and peaceful way whatever days God still allotted him.

I saw another face of aging in America on Saturday mornings when I went on my paper route collection calls. One stop was at a privately run nursing home in a converted house. In order to get my money, I had to go from the front porch back through a series of rooms to the kitchen, where the owner's wife was usually at work preparing meals for the twenty or so residents, or should I say inmates. I was perhaps eleven years old, and the sight of so many old and obviously unhappy people crowded together under very questionable conditions was unnerving. I would try to breathe as infrequently as possible, for aging has an odor, at least it did in the Ahrens Nursing Home. Many years later when I was at college, mother wrote that the Ahrens Nursing Home had been closed by state authorities for violations of assorted ordinances. I was not surprised.

You are doubtless thinking that these are very maudlin reflections for one who is approaching only his fiftieth birthday. I expect to go full tilt at life for a good long while yet, despite graying and thinning hair and a few other early warning signs of election to senior citizen status. But out there somewhere is a computer that has my name in it which has been sending me junk mail soliciting the purchase of subscriptions to retirement magazines, garden carts one can sit on to weed, and God forbid, even those mechanized contour chairs that Art Linkletter pitches. From the perspective of the computer, I am simply one of millions of Americans who will be at or near retirement age by the end of this century. In the aggregate at least, I am, like many of you, one of those liabilities that the Social Security system will carry with it into the year 2000 and beyond.

Gerontology is an academic discipline in American universities which focuses on the study of the aging process and attendant social problems. It is of fairly recent origin in African universities, for the elderly are only now being thought of as in need of special consideration. Under the impact of urbanization, the young worldwide are migrating from rural areas to the cities, leaving the elderly in the traditional villages without support. I am told that many of the values and customs that once put the old in positions of honor are under stress, as they are in China and other non-western cultures undergoing modernization. In the United States we must contend with an aging population that will need adequate housing, better health care, and a host of other supportive agencies. That won't happen until as a culture we restore the value of respect and honor for the elderly that the youth-targeted media merchants undercut at every turn.

Churches can play an important role in making the elderly feel part of the community. I have noticed that new churches now are accessible to those in wheelchairs and that existing structures have added ramps and other facilities so that the elderly can feel welcome. Churches must do more, beginning with a self-conscious effort to educate all members about the continuum of life from the babe in the crib to the old man or woman in the hospital bed. In many respects the very old among us are like the very young, dependent upon our assistance and in need of our genuine and unqualified love. The church may be the one sanctuary that the elderly can call their own.

On my fortieth birthday, my brother and I went up to the Adirondacks and climbed Algonquin, one of the high peaks. I thought of it then as a middle-age challenge, though the mosquitoes were more of an obstacle than the mountain. I am not sure what one does when marking a half-century of existence and am open to suggestions. Perhaps a walk along the Erie Canal towpath is in order.

Postscript: Now, twenty years later, I turn 70 this July 21, 2012. I have a new (and expensive) pair of hearing aids. There is less hair to blow in the wind. I have lived more years than either my father, grandfather, or great grandfather did. I hope to reach the biblical fourscore years (80) as in Psalm 90:10--" The days of our years are threescore years and ten; and if by reason of strength they be fourscore years, yet is their strength labour and sorrow; for it is soon cut off, and we fly away." --without all of the labour and sorrow the Psalmist wrote of and I hope that the church and the community are ready for me (and all of us who are part of an aging America).

August 2012

The Hat

"Gratia Dei sum quod sum." 1 Corinthians 15: 10

John Updike's memoir, appropriately titled Self-Consciousness, makes for interesting summer reading. This Pulitzer Prize winning writer of more than three dozen books, including <u>Rabbit Run</u> (1960) and <u>The Witches of Eastwick</u> (1984), was born in 1932 in Shillington, Pennsylvania, and attended the basement Sunday school of Grace Lutheran Church. Throughout his life, Updike has been painfully self-conscious, a self-consciousness compounded by psoriasis and stuttering. Updike's remarkable revelatory memoir contains countless examples of one who is, as Updike divulges, "precociously conscious of the precious, inexplicable burden of selfhood." "Burden" is exactly the right

73

word, for self-consciousness has its price. Embarrassed, we withdraw, we limit, and we hide.

Updike's over-sensitive inner gyroscope tilted whenever his father, a high school mathematics teacher, wore a blue knitted Navy watch cap that made him look "like a cretin." Updike worked the watch cap into The Centaur (1963) where the young boy Peter is embarrassed by the cap his father wears. "Pulled down over his ears, it made him look like an overgrown dimwit in a comic strip." Toward the end of his memoir, Updike reveals that at age sixty-plus he too wears a watch cap like his father's, indoors as well as outdoors, despite his wife's conviction that he looks foolish. "I discover," Updike says, "that there is no pain and a certain pleasure in looking foolish. Looking foolish does the spirit good. The need not to look foolish is one of youth's many burdens [that] as we get older we are exempted from more and more, and float upward in our heedlessness, singing Gratia Dei sum quod sum (By the Grace of God, I am what I am)."

I almost "get" the theory of relativity, but I cannot understand why teenagers can don outlandish garb and yet approach emotional meltdown when their parents dress out of character. My brother-in-law was an electrical engineer for the National Space Administration in New Mexico and a man with no known vices, with the possible exception of golf and a habit of braking at the last-second prior to a red light. We call them "Uncle Don stops." He is even-tempered, reliable, and a good father. There are times, however, when even the best of fathers proves to be an embarrassment to their offspring. I was in Las Cruces, New Mexico, many years ago to attend my nephew's high school graduation. All went smoothly until after the ceremonies when we decided to drive up into the mountains. New Mexico is the land of the perpetual sun, so my brother-in-law wisely brought along a wide-brimmed straw hat, decorated with fish (Or was it birds?). I thought he appeared appropriately festive in the hat, but his son had conniptions. Updike thought his dad looked "like a cretin" in that Navy watch cap. I think my nephew used the word "dorky" to refer to his dad's headgear. He was so upset that a mini-battle broke out in the car as we were driving along, with the son grabbing the dad's hat, the dad grabbing it back, and the son grabbing it again until my sister wisely called a halt to the whole business for the safety of us all.

When I was young and in Sunday school at Trinity Lutheran Church, Hampton, Iowa, hats were in. After services, winter and summer, there was a parting of the congregation as it exited the nave. The adult males trooped down the stairs to the basement in order to retrieve their hats from above the coat racks, while the women waited in the narthex, or if the weather permitted, went out on the steps and exchanged family news. They, following the custom among conservative Lutherans in those days, had been required to cover their heads during worship. Sometimes I would lose my mother's hand and be swept along with the male tide, down the stairs, into that cloakroom. That was my initiation into the male Lutheran club, with its talk of weather and crops and the smell of an occasional after-church cigar. Fatherless by the age of seven, I looked to these Lutheran elders rummaging for their hats as the guardians of the moral order in our corner of the world and thought of the hat as the symbol of their authority. Then I grew up; hats for men went out of fashion; and Lutheranism and life seemed to become more complicated and less of a sure thing.

I am not arguing that Lutheranism and other mainstream denominations, including the United Methodist Church, have declined because of the disappearance of the hat, though the shelves above the coat hangers at our church in Cazenovia are mostly hatless. Nor do I urge the reintroduction of the gender gap during worship. But something must be said for the hat--any hat, especially the foolish hat. My own collection of caps runs mostly toward the agricultural, with logos like "AgriPro" and "John Deere." I have not yet placed any hats on the deck of the rear window of our car as Baptists do, mostly Southern Baptists. I am, however, risking a little silliness as I get older, sport a billed cap indoors, and may some day be bold enough to declare Gratia Dei sum quod sum and wear one of my corniest hats to church.

It will be my testimony to the grace of God, to the proposition that silliness can be redemptive because, truth be told, we are children of grace.

Postscript: Last month at the chicken barbecue, Bill Goodfellow, Bob Arnold, and several other trusty stewards of the great cook off, called my attention to a solitary hat, a nice looking one with a chin strap and ear flaps, sitting by the church exit. Thinking it mine, they urged me to take it home. I tried it on; it gave me a Crocodile Dundee look! But when I got home, I discovered that the hat (size medium) didn't belong to me and have, to clear my conscience, returned it to church. I am, however, missing a fine felt green fedora. Perhaps some hat wearer out there is now sporting it as his (or her) testimony to the notion that a little silliness can be redemptive.

"But by the grace of God I am what I am: and his grace which was bestowed upon me was not found vain; but I labored more abundantly than they all: yet not I, but the grace of God which was with me." 1 Corinthians 15:10

September 2012

What Makes You Special?

In March of 2003, yours truly had a bone scan as one of the tests needed prior to surgery for prostate cancer. This was my first trip through a high tech machine that uses x-rays to produce a picture of the human skeleton. When I was done with the 45-minute procedure, the technician called me over to look at the photographic image. What a disappointment! While I was pleased to find out that the cancer had not spread into my skeletal structures, I was disappointed in what I saw. My skeleton was nothing special. It reminded me of the one that stood in Mr. Newman's 9th-grade science class during my high school years. That skeleton had no name, though some kids called him "Mr. Bones."

I am not sure what I expected or exactly why the bone scan was such a downer. I suspect that I was naively looking for something on the scan that defined the essential me, that unique quality of self that the baby born on July 21, 1942, at the Lutheran Hospital in Hampton, Iowa, has come to possess.

Where was that incredible essence of "me-ness" that I have long believed differentiates Milton Charles Sernett from the millions? All of us grow up thinking of ourselves as one-of-a-kind, as if God were a divine potter and threw away the mold after making us. It was a humbling experience to discover, as far as that scanning machine was concerned, that I was just another bag of bones.

My surgery took place on May 19, 2003 in Chicago at Northwestern Hospital. While waiting at O'Hara airport for our return flight to Syracuse, I picked up a copy of Time magazine. It featured an article on the question of what makes you who you are. The authors reviewed the ancient debate about the relative influence of nature and nurture in shaping the individual. Partisans of the nature argument, such as Immanuel Kant and Noam Chomsky, believe that individuality can be reduced to innate and pre-determined characteristics. Time summed up the nature position as follows: "We may be destined to be bald, mourn our dead, seek mates, fear the dark." The nurture advocates, such as Ivan Pavlov and Sigmund Freud, stressed the importance of environment and culture upon the individual. As Time put it, "But we can also learn to love tea, hate polkas, invent alphabets and tell lies."

The nature vs. nurture debate is an old one. What apparently makes a discussion of it newsworthy now is a theory arising out of the human genome project about how genes in the human DNA blueprint get switched on and off. I do not pretend to understand the technical specifics. However, it appears that the latest research suggests that genes are not static, but respond to changes in the environment in the womb. In simpler terms, nature and nurture interact to shape the DNA text of each distinct individual. I am not sure that this new understanding of genes will put the perennial nature vs. nurture argument to rest. The human mind loves dichotomies.

While I found the Time article interesting, it did not resolve the fundamental question posed by my bone scan. I have long been partial to the nurture argument, so it was comforting to read that the hard-nosed geneticists who believe that the DNA code holds the answer to what distinguishes the man (or woman) from the mouse are willing to acknowledge that nurture plays a role too. Nevertheless, my own search for what makes me special (and you the reader special too) did not show up in that magazine article.

Do you remember what Pastor Robin told us last month on Assumption Sunday? Life has its "Aha" moments, those experiences that forever alter our way of looking at ourselves in relation to others and to God. I had an "Aha!" or "I get it!" experience on Friday, May 23, 2003, at about 4:30 P.M. in a room on the 23rd floor of the Fitzpatrick Hotel in downtown Chicago. I was lying in bed, suffering from a post-surgical backache that would make a nun swear. About twenty minutes earlier, Dr. William J. Catalona, my surgeon, had phoned with the good news that the final pathology report showed that the cancer had not spread beyond the prostate and that he had gotten "clean margins." Jan and I had shared a moment of rejoicing and she resumed her needlepoint project, putting on head phones to listen to a CD of hymns recorded by the Washington National Choir. Suddenly my wife broke out in song, albeit slightly off key, as one is wont to do when singing with headphones on. A rush of warmth came over me, drowning out the back pain. I discovered what I had not seen on that bone scan. I was me—a unique me—because I was loved.

You are special because of the circle of family and friends who care about you. Their love reflects and has its source in God's love for you. In Christian Baptism, God has called you by name, calling you out from the masses, making you too one-of-a-kind!

October 2012

A Short Course in Christian Continuing Education

No need to hike to Vermont this October when you only need to look out the window for beautiful fall colors. Each year when our trees (all except the conifers) start to turn, I try to recall how it is that fall foliage arrives with such a rich palette of reds, oranges, purples and yellows. In addition, every fall someone has to explain to me why the leaves change color. Here it is in simple form.

Leaves are little food factories. Mr. Chlorophyll (who is green) runs the show, taking energy from the sun. He gobbles up carbon dioxide and water, and produces sugars and starches, needed by plants to grow. When the days shorten and Mr. Sun winters in Orlando, Florida, Mr. Chlorophyll takes a holiday break. Green recedes, and the yellow to orange colors step forward. Some of you who did better in high school biology than I will know about those red anthocyanin pigments that dress dogwoods and sumacs in darker colors, reds and purples. Remember, I became a historian, not a professor of environmental science.

Science and nature hold many mysteries. For example, I don't understand why the sky is blue or how the Internet can bring me the sound of a live concert from a Scottish cathedral on my computer, which I can then play on my home sound system as the musicians perform! Given my lack of sophistication in anything having to do with electricity, do not ask me to describe the duties of Mr. Watt, Mr. Ohm, or Mr. Volt. For all I know, these three could be a pop singing group. I worry about the poor state of my scientific knowledge. I fear it makes me too gullible, too likely to believe nonsense parading as science. Here's an example:

When a cat is dropped it always lands on its feet. When buttered toast is dropped it always lands with the buttered side facing down. If a piece of buttered toast were attached to the back of a cat, when dropped, the cat & buttered toast combination should hover, spinning just above the ground, as it tries unsuccessfully to resolve the inevitable conflict of non-scientific certainties.

This in itself might be fun to watch, but there is a serious point to be made here. What if giant arrangements of buttered toast cats were linked (probably by their tails) to banks of generators? Perhaps enough electricity could be produced to help resolve the growing world energy crisis.

It is said that necessity is the mother of invention. I will need energy this winter, so I'm tempted to test the theory that buttered toast cats could be used to make electricity. Science utilizes the experimental method. I could get three cats, butter, bread, and a toaster. Should I give it a go? I may not know a watt from an ohm, but I know enough about electricity to label the buttered-toast cat theory "silly science."

There is a lot of silly theology being pushed these days. Far too many Christians are taken in because ignorance produces gullibility. Unfortunately, good Christian education programs languish. Many adults feel that they can go through life equipped only with what they learned in Sunday school and Confirmation classes. Their theological training stopped a long time ago, but their lives haven't.

During October, Lutherans and Protestant Christians (including Methodists) worldwide celebrate Martin Luther's discovery of the fundamental teaching of the Christian faith: *Sola Fidei* -- "Justification by Faith Alone." Luther would not have recovered this essential Christian doctrine had he not been a lifelong learner, even when armed with an earned doctorate in theology from the University of Wittenberg. In my mind's eye, I always picture Luther holding a book, or, when not reading or teaching, writing one of his own. When I was much younger than I am now, I once thought of putting the 55-volume set of Luther's Works, the monumental collection edited by Jaroslav Pelikan and published jointly by Concordia Publishing House and Fortress Press in 1957, on my Christmas wish list. I deferred. Too expensive and too bulky to tote around. Now Luther's many writings are on CD-ROM. $219.95 on sale! I am tempted but a wiser voice (my wife) says no. You can go to the library for this stint in Christian Continuing Education.

One does not need to read all of Luther's writings to learn from him. Christians, he teaches us, must be lifelong students of God's word. By doing so, we equip ourselves to do battle with the silly theologies of the twenty-first century just as the German monk who defied both emperor and pope for the sake of God's truth did in the sixteenth century.

I find it hard to shed my Lutheran identity. Odd as it may seem, there are no Lutheran churches in all of Madison County, so our church home is now the United Methodist Church of Cazenovia. This is right, fitting, and proper.

For did not John Wesley, the spiritual father of Methodism, come to a deeper understanding of God's grace in 1738 at Aldersgate while hearing a reading of Luther's preface to the Epistle to the Romans. Here is what Wesley wrote in his Journal on May 24, 1738:

In the evening I went very unwillingly to a society in Aldersgate Street, where one was reading Luther's preface to the Epistle to the Romans. About a quarter before nine, while the leader was describing the change which God works in the heart through faith in Christ, I felt my heart strangely warmed. I felt I did trust in Christ alone for salvation; and an assurance was given me that He had taken away my sins, even mine, and saved me from the law of sin and death.

November 2012

On Being the Apple of God's Eye

Were the world to end tomorrow and I had but one tree to save, it would be the apple tree. My fondness for the apple is rooted in memories of old farm orchards and fall afternoons stirring hot apple butter with a wooden spoon in a big blue enamel bowl back in Iowa. Unfortunately, the apple crop here in Central New York this year was not as bountiful as in other years. Perhaps it is time to plant an apple tree or two in my backyard.

John Chapman (1775-1845) chose a most noble vocation in planting apple orchards in advance of the first settlers in Ohio, Indiana, and elsewhere. Thus did he earn the nickname "Johnny Appleseed" and a niche in American folk history. Few Americans, however, know that Chapman's apple-tree enthusiasm was rivaled only by his desire to circulate Christian tracts among the scattered cabins on the frontier. Chapman's devotion to the apple tree had a mystical quality to it, perhaps because he was a disciple of Emmanuel Swedenborg, an 18th-century Swedish mystic and religious philosopher.

Thus it has always troubled me that the apple's reputation has been bruised by association with the story of the Fall in Genesis 3. Sunday school pictures common to my generation showed Eve taking an apple from the Tree of the Knowledge of Good and Evil. Never mind that the Biblical account does not identify what kind of botanical specimen stood in the middle of the Garden of Eden. Everyone assumes that it was an apple tree. Not a crabapple tree, mind you, or some weird-tasting fruit like the avocado or persimmon, but a beautiful red apple like the kind I used to take to school in my battered Roy Rogers lunch pail.

At last I have public space to defend the good name of the apple tree. Proverbs 25: 11 says, "A word fitly spoken is like apples of gold in baskets of silver." Let it be known that in at least five Old Testament passages there is an emphasis on how God's chosen people were the apple of His eye. Israel had been selected from among all the nations of the earth, its prophets said, to stand in a special covenant relation with God.

From the lineage of Abraham, Isaac, and Jacob, the Messiah would one day come. Yet, as the plea in Lamentations 2: 18 ("... let not the apple of thine eye cease") suggests, God's chosen people nearly came to destruction because they had forgotten the covenant. At times they acted more like the apple of Sodom, a fruit described by ancient writers as externally of fair appearance but dissolving into smoke and ashes when plucked. So the Psalmist (17:8) cried out: "Keep me as the apple of thine eye; hide me under the shadow of thy wings."

We of the New Israel by faith in Jesus Christ can take comfort in the promise that we are highly cherished by God. This "apple-of-His-eye" relationship, however, places special responsibilities upon us. Like Johnny Appleseed, we are to leave behind some evidence of having passed along the road of life, some faith-seedling that will bear fruit to nourish those who will follow. The apple-cability of this is that each of us witness to the Lord Jesus Christ in whatever place we are.

Have a bountiful and thankful Thanksgiving!

December 2012

An Old Story Retold

When our daughter was small and dwelt in the land of the imagination, I coveted the half hour between bedtime and sleep time. Then it was that I became the spinner of tales, weaving elaborate stories about a little blue bird for Rebecca. Part of the joy was in the telling, for I prepared not a wit and each night took a simple theme and embellished it with no notion of where I would end up. It was as if the spirit of the blue bird powered the narrative, and I was only an oracle through whom this other force spoke. Many years have come and gone. Rebecca's childhood days are but memory, and yet that little blue bird is inside my head, waiting I suppose for another willing listener.

Good storytelling is an art. The old, familiar stories are the most difficult to retell. That of the Birth of Jesus is often called "The Greatest Story Ever Told." "In those days a decree went out from Caesar Augustus." Familiar words. We can recite them from memory-- for we have heard St. Luke's account of the Christmas narrative a hundred times in sermon and in song. Therein lies the storyteller's burden. Year in and year out the tale is the same. Mary, Joseph, the Baby Jesus. Same cast of characters. Same setting. Same plot. Even the extras are old hands. The shepherds never fail to be "filled with fear" when the angel tells them "for you is born this day in the city of David a savior, who is Christ the Lord." Why the surprise, I ask, when they have the same thing happen to them every year? And what about those Three So-Called Wise Men? You would think they would have their parts down pat by now and one of these Nativity Festivals get to the manger on time rather than waiting until Epiphany.

In a world characterized by change and impermanence, it is comforting to hear the Christmas story just as we first came to know it. Year in and year out, God's love is recapitulated for us in the chronicle of the Incarnation just as we first came to know the story when small and yet uncertain as to the meaning of it all. Older children, like most adults, can tell you when it was that the Santa Claus story was demythologized for them. Perhaps it was when on the same December afternoon they saw Santa driving a Syracuse bus downtown and another Santa greeting kids at the shopping mall and they declared that the man in the red suit was a hoax. Does it work the other way? Can you recall when or how it was that the Christmas narrative became far more than a story about a baby in a manger, some bewildered shepherds, and an angel or two? How do adults keep alive the mystery and the power of a story so often told and so familiar?

I'm not sure that I have the answer, but I've found a clue in a moving story told by Bob Artley in his book *Ginny: A Love Remembered.* It tells of his fifty-year love affair with Virginia Elnore Moore and of the debilitating effects of Alzheimer's from which "Ginny" suffered in her last  years. Bob Artley (1917-2011) was an award-winning editorial cartoonist who worked many years for the Des Moines *Tribune.* Toward the end of his career he began to publish in cartoon form reflections of growing up in the 1920s and 1930s on the family farm near my hometown of Hampton, Iowa. I became an avid collector of those my mother clipped and sent me and of the cartoon anthologies Artley published under such titles as *Memories of a Former Kid.*

In *Country Christmas: As Remembered by a Former Kid*, Artley depicts with vivid detail the pleasures of preparing for Christmas as seen through the eyes of a young boy on an Iowa farm. His father makes wooden freight train cars in the farm workshop. Mom Artley bakes delicious pies, cakes, cookies, popcorn balls, and special homemade candy on the big old-fashioned kitchen range. And Bob and his brothers go about their chores whistling Christmas carols and giving the cows and pigs extra corn as "Christmas treats." In the large two-story farm house there stands a spruce tree decorated with tinfoil-covered cardboard stars, strings of popcorn and cranberries, and paper chains. The scene is one of unadulterated happiness.

Flash forward some six decades. Bob has retired from professional cartooning; "let go" would be a better word. When the *Worthington Daily Globe* in Minnesota, where he launched his "Memories of a Former Kid" series, changed hands, cutbacks were made and Bob was one of the casualties. In 1979 Ginny, who had been operating the family's small printing business, began to have trouble coping with the details of her work. She was diagnosed with Alzheimer's disease in 1982, a year after the couple moved back to Hampton, Iowa. In 1985, the Artleys returned to the farm where Bob grew up. Ginny was to spend one family Christmas there. Artley writes, "Many Christmases had been celebrated in this old farmhouse. My first memories of Christmas had been of this place, where the love and magic and wonder had first become real to me, coloring all the subsequent Christmases through the years. . . .. As we planned for the first Christmas our family had experienced in this house for several years, we all knew it would be Ginny's last there." In 1987 Ginny had to be placed in the Iowa Veterans Home. She died there in 1993. Reading of Bob Artley's love and devotion for Ginny, who at the end did not recognize him as her husband, against the backdrop of his earlier recollections of a child's view of Christmas, made the old story come alive again. Perhaps that is the miracle of Christmas.

January 2013

Looking for Happiness in the New Year?

People look for happiness in the strangest places. When in Wegman's grocery store with wife and son some years back, I wandered over to the stand alone computer one touches to locate odd items like Tofu and Tangerines. It was late on a workday, we were weary of grocery shopping, and I was anxious to get home on one of those cold winter nights typical of upstate New York in January. Moved by curiosity or perhaps it was out of boredom, I pushed the buttons on the "Looking for Something?" machine and scrolled down to locate Happiness. It was not to be found. Its nearest neighbors were Handi-wipes and Hardware. Now the handiwipe is a marvelous invention, as any mother of a messy two-year old knows, and I can spend an hour blissfully browsing the aisles of a well-stocked hardware store, but neither commodity is the equal of happiness.

Each new year brings a blank ledger to our lives. The sum total of the next twelve months is yet to be determined, and no one, prophet or seer, can divine its pluses and minuses. The year past has the virtue of the known, but the one to come carries in its uncertainty a nagging anxiety regarding the future. The makers of things know this and try to sell us happiness in commodities from A to Z. Advertisers promote a vision of the good life built upon the accumulation of stuff, as if contentment could be purchased with WIZ bucks at zero interest for twelve months. The truth is that things rust out, wear out, and with the passage of time cross into the category of junk, as a survey of your typical neighborhood garage sale this spring will demonstrate.

What is to be done? I found a useful remedy for life's perennial discontent in a "Reflections" column in a magazine appropriately called Mature Outlook and sent to those of us of senior citizen status. The writer had asked her readers to send in memories of their mothers under the theme "I remember mama." Mary Fran Purse of Northfield, Illinois submitted the following:

"Mother was 'Matey' (for Mater) to all of us. She never could enjoy simple pleasures alone--she needed to share them. 'Someone! Just come out and see the sunset!' she'd cry. And although the response was often, 'Oh Matey, you and your sunsets,' we'd come. Our favorite story concerns a fire in a kitchen wastebasket, which someone was about to douse with a bucket of water. Matey dashed off, shouting, 'Don't put it out till the baby sees it!' Matey knew the secret of finding true happiness."

Scroll down between Small and Shared on your personal "Looking for Something?" computer. Happiest are those who take joy in what money cannot buy--a beautiful sunset, the smile of the baby--Mother Matey's delight in the serendipitous. Matey's passion for life apparently derived from her notion that all things wonderful must be shared. She knew too that small can be beautiful.

When our son Matthew was at the tadpole stage his mother and I would take him on afternoon walks around the block at our old place in Syracuse. Matt was then just discovering the world outside and so would wander down the sidewalk gathering up bits of this and that--his treasures. At wash time Jan would rescue Matt's collection of pebbles, wacky sticks, Cicada carcasses, dirty pennies, and most anything else before all went down the drain. The ability to take pleasure in the ordinary belongs to the young--before they are corrupted by adult purveyors of the philosophy that more is better. And the young, like Mother Matey, have this instinctive need to share what in their eyes is beautiful. "Look Mom," "Look Dad" is their constant cry. Sometimes we tire of their incessant demand that we enjoy what they enjoy and brush them off with "That's nice." In so doing, we distance ourselves from the wellspring of authentic happiness.

In 1990 I had the good fortune of meeting the Scottish vet known by his pen name as James Herriot, author of books and subject of a popular television series. Then retired, Herriot came in on some afternoons to his old practice there in Thirsk in the Yorkshire Dales. I waited in line with other fans, feeling a bit uneasy. I am always uncomfortable around celebrities and would make a poor rock star groupie. Fame and fortune can be intimidating. Herriot graciously welcomed us strangers. Surrounded by mementos of his lifelong love of animals and people, he apologized for giving us book plates with autographs he had laboriously penned out at home. Arthritis, caused by spending many nights in nights in cold barns and more recently of too much book signing, crippled his right hand. I was struck with the authentic nature of the man. He was content, having learned a long time ago that happiness is not a commodity but God's precious gift. And so he wrote of:

All things bright and beautiful,
All creatures great and small,
All things wise and wonderful,
The Lord God made them all.

February 2013

God's Shoe Box of Love

When young and shy I dreaded the approach of Valentine's Day. To be a second grader with a shoe box and very little in it by way of hand-crafted tokens of love from one's classmates brought no end of  regret. Some teachers mandated that each student make a Valentine for every member of the class, assuring equity and no hurt feelings. Mine let us fend for ourselves. The law of popularity (and its inverse) ruled; some children gave more than they received. Mrs. McMan apparently believed that we would profit from a lesson in one of the facts of life. We should know how to cope with rejection. Then when we became adults, we would strive to create community and love where none existed.

We live in the age of identity politics. Individuals group themselves in ideological and social conflict against other groups along lines of race, class, gender, religion, place of abode, food preferences, cultural fads, musical tastes, party politics, age, etc. There is no end to ways in which humans divide themselves into categories. Then they start suing one another and, in the end, the lawyers profit the most.

I began to reflect on the theme of community while attending the wedding reception of my niece Kelly in Austin, Texas. I had been asked to give the blessing before the banquet and did so by remarking that I couldn't give the one I had improvised for the reception dinner a year or so earlier in Michigan where another of my nieces, Kate Sernett, was married. Then I had asked the Lord to protect Kate and her new husband Kim as they journeyed by U-Haul truck to Texas- "a far and distant land where they will be living among strangers and Baptists!" This line drew smiles from the largely Lutheran audience in Michigan, for Lutherans know Texas and the South to be "Baptist country." I did not think my one-liner would go over well at the Austin reception and said so. Indeed, later on my daughter commented that one of the Baptist young friends of the bride had not understood the joke to begin with. I guess one has to have at least a journeyman's knowledge of American religious history and of the denominational spatial patterns that emerged after 1776 and still exist today. Ask any Southern Baptist preacher who has tried to set up shop up here in the North and he will tell you how it feels to be a stranger in a "far and distant land."

Weddings are highly symbolic occasions and we resonate at some deep level to the call to unity given by the preacher to the bride and groom. The vows are spoken, rings exchanged, and two individuals (and their families) are joined together– "until death do us part." Then the wedding photographer goes to work. A good wedding photographer must be professional and unobtrusive, blending technical skill with the high art of diplomacy. My niece Kelly lucked out. The woman behind the camera orchestrated all of us adroitly, not only at the church but also later at the reception. Once she had exhausted the natural groupings (bride and groom, wedding party, parents of the groom, parents of the bride, etc.), she roamed the banquet hall and dance floor for other possible photographic opportunities. At one point, she called me away from the table where I sat to pose me in a setting she referred to as "fathers with daughters." I jokingly asked her, "What's next? Four people who met in a mall?"

Now that I have had time to reflect, I regret being so flip. We hunger for community in these times when the forces of division (ranging from identity politics to armed conflict) trouble the world. Let us celebrate community and the many and varied ways in which individuals try to foster fellowship. Join and belong; be part of something larger than yourself. That too has been the American way. How else to explain such groups as the Loyal Order of the Moose and St. Agnes's Thursday night bingo club? I'm even beginning to think better of organizations in which the individuals have nothing more in common other than ownership of an Airstream Camper or a Harley Davidson motorcycle. I am looking for a group of John Deere 870 tractor enthusiasts. We'll hold mowing and snow plowing contests and then ride our green machines together doing square dance patterns down Main Street.

The Biblical story of sin and redemption is fundamentally about the Valentine that God gave the world. In Christ Jesus we have become one family, one community of the twice born, a fellowship forged in unconditional love. Our identity as children of God transcends all that would divide us. That is the promise, but as with the wedding vows exchanged between bride and groom, we have to work at keeping our commitments all of our days. Southern Baptists speak of "back sliding" because they know of sin and disappointment. But they also give witness to Amazing Grace because God delivers us from our separateness and our sinfulness. So I am grateful for my sojourn into Baptist country and for being reminded by the wedding photographer that community (no matter how transitory) is God's way of making sure that each of our shoe boxes is full of tokens of love.

March 2013

Highway to Heaven

Christians worldwide celebrate Easter at the end of this month and proclaim the radical good news that "He is Alive." I sometimes wonder how we can do this in a culture where the Resurrection message bumps up against widespread theological ignorance and a thick wall of religious foolishness. Consider the implications of a survey conducted by ABC news in which 47 per cent of pet owners said that their pet (dog, cat, hamster, fish or ferret) would go to heaven. Thirty-eight per cent of non-pet owners agreed.

The survey reminded me of the animated film "All Dogs Go to Heaven," a 1989 production in which a German Shepherd (voiced by Burt Reynolds) dies and goes to Heaven. According to the scriptwriters, all dogs go to Heaven because "unlike people, dogs are naturally good and loyal and kind." I have never owned a dog and hesitate to generalize about the species. I do have difficulty accepting the premise that all dogs are "naturally good and loyal and kind." When I was a paperboy and delivered the Mason City Globe-Gazette, ill-tempered pooches of varying breeds and sizes routinely chased me down the street, nipping at my feet as I furiously pedaled away on my bike.

We have owned a series of cats. We had to have our three elderly felines, whom no pet shelter would accept, "put to sleep" (note the euphemism). Our granddaughter Amanda had developed such an allergic reaction to them that the doctors recommended putting her on steroids. Well-meaning folks offered us condolences, with remarks such as "There is a special place for cats in Heaven," or words to that effect. My inner voice responded, "I don't think so. Those cats are probably in the Madison County landfill."

My pet-loving but unsentimental self approaches this month's observance of the Easter story with renewed conviction that Christians need to hold firm to the Biblical teaching about the radical uniqueness of Jesus' resurrection from the dead. The Apostle Paul emphasized this centuries ago: "And if Christ has not been raised, our preaching is useless and so is your faith. More than that, we are then found to be false witnesses about God, for we have testified about God that he raised Christ from the dead. But he did not raise him if in fact the dead are not raised." (1 Corinthians 15:14-15)

Perhaps many people today miss the full majesty and power of the Open Tomb because they stumble at the Cross. Like the script writers for "All Dogs Go to Heaven" who operated from the premise of canine universalism, the easy temptation is to want to take a detour around Golgotha and the suffering and death of Jesus and go straight to Easter's message that the Risen Christ has conquered the powers of hell and taken the sting out of death. Some religious thinkers have argued since God is good, everyone gets a free pass to Heaven. If that were so, then the Cross at Calvary was a mockery at best and a divine hoax at worst. There can be no Crown without the Cross.

The Westminster Kennel Club Dog Show is the premier dog show of the canine season, where pedigree is everything and the stakes are high (monetary and otherwise). The handlers show the Working Dog breeds, such as the Great Pyrenees, the Neapolitan Mastiff, and the Doberman Pinscher. The Komondor looks like a giant white mop, though it is supposed to have descended from a fierce working dog native to Hungary. Like many of the other pooches in the Working Dog class, the Komondor has been domesticated and dandified for the Westminster show. Not much of the old Hungarian livestock guard dog remains in him anymore.

I see an analogy here. For some people, Easter is mostly about Easter lilies, dye-colored eggs, bunnies, and bright-colored clothes. Our culture has domesticated Easter, muting its astounding proclamation that the highway to Heaven begins at the foot of the Cross on Good Friday and is made possible because of the Open Tomb. Ten million cats and dogs are said to be lost every year in the United States. As a pet lover (though presently not a pet owner), this statistic tugs at the heart. How much more ought we to be heartsick over those fellow mortals who, for whatever reason, have yet to share in the joyful celebration of the Easter affirmation that Jesus is the Victorious One!

I fear that this month's Reflections essay will bring me grief. Dog lovers will wag their fingers at me in disapproval, sure that their pet is a candidate for dog heaven. Cat owners will chastise me for believing that the Madison County landfill, or its equivalent, is the end of the road for aged felines.

In my defense, I offer this thought to advocates of the "all dogs get to Heaven" brand of theology. The Westminster show commentator once said, "There are no bad dogs, only bad owners." If that is true, think of the consequences. If Waldo, your Fox Terrier, gets to Heaven and you do not, then who is going to look after him? A silly surmise, of course, but this is what happens when we domesticate Easter and get diverted from the truth of John 14:6.

Jesus said,

"I am the Way and the Truth and the Life. No one comes to the Father except through Me."

April 2013

Warble On!

Elojia Macias loves to sing. Fellow worshipers do not care for her unique way of doing so. According to a press report, the members of Our Lady of Sorrows Catholic Church in San Antonio took her to court. She was charged with causing "confusion and disruption" in worship by singing her own songs. Despite pleas from Father Wangler and dirty looks by the dozen, Ms. Macias warbled on, singing first from the pew, then going up to the sound system and using it. In the lawsuit, the overzealous songstress was charged with causing the church a "loss of good will, spiritual tranquility and membership." Judge John Specia placed an injunction on Macias. Should she sing again in such a disruptive manner, she was to be charged with contempt of court. I have no clue as to what happened at 9 a.m. mass on the following Sunday. Newspapers dropped the story.

How would the Cazenovia United Methodist Church have handled the matter? Let's assume that Ms. Macias had a good voice, or a reasonable facsimile thereof. Should she have been muzzled? Catholics in the pew prior to Vatican II, when the liturgy was in Latin in conservative circles, rarely sang in unison. Perhaps we can forgive the members of Our Lady of Sorrows because of their inexperience with congregational hymnody. Insecure in their abilities, they picked upon the individualist. But Methodists churches are known as singing churches, given the legacy of hymn writers such as Charles Wesley. Surely we could find a place for another songbird.

I come out of the Lutheran tradition. When a member of Faith Lutheran Church, Cicero, I was active in the choir. When I sang loudly, my fourteen-year old son threw daggers my way or, if sitting in the pew with him, poked me in the side. He was embarrassed by my vocalizations. I could not understand it. My voice was once good enough, though I am no longer able to reach the tenor notes of my college choir days. I suspect my hearing. When my right ear took a vacation, I could no longer pick out the correct note in a chord and had to rely on the person standing next to me. Lately, my hearing has deteriorated to the point where even this technique produces uncertain results. I have taken a sabbatical from choir duty so as not to embarrass r myself. Nevertheless, I plan to sing the melodies of hymns as loudly as ever with the rest of the congregation and hope that I will not meet the fate of Elojia Macias.

Though I put away my choir book long ago, I have a great fondness for those good folks who week-to-week contribute to our worship service in such a special way. I applaud songbirds such as Chip McEvers, Carol Gravelding, and, of course, our own Pastor Robin. They sing with enthusiasm and more talent than I can muster. That on any given Sunday they may not sound like the world famous Salt Lake City choir is more a matter of numbers than talent or commitment. Multiply their efforts a hundred fold and you have the Mormon Tabernacle Choir.

Some years ago we were visiting good friends who live in Amish country in southeastern Pennsylvania and joined them in worship at the Middle Octorora Presbyterian Church, now more than two hundred years old. A small choir, perhaps only seven or eight strong, offered several selections. As they sat together near the front of the chancel, I had plenty of time to observe them during the pastor's sermon. What an assortment of humanity they were--tall/short, skinny/not-so-skinny, young/old, male/female, and many other variations. One elderly gentleman looked like a character from Charles Dickens' "Christmas Carol." Another choir member wore a sport jacket that could have stopped a locomotive. A very large lady served as the director, while my friend's wife played the organ. Suddenly all my reservations vanished. This odd assortment of Christians could sing! It was as if they were angels in disguise. One ought not to judge a church choir by its size or appearance. God gives voice to those who really care.

Join me then in a salute to all those who volunteer to offer "special music" during our worship services. Like small church choirs everywhere, they may occasionally hit a sour note but the sum of their hard work is sweet indeed. Warble on, good folks.

May 2013

Go Fish!

Visit Baltimore's Lexington Market and eat at Mrs. Faidley's restaurant. She serves up great seafood and posts a sign that reads: "Note that Jesus fed the crowd, not fatty beef, not greasy lamb, not sausage or salami. He fed them loaves and fishes. He knew what was good for them."

Nearly two thousand years ago, at a time when the early Christians lived dangerously if they openly professed their faith during Roman rule, believers took to drawing the symbol of a fish to identify themselves to fellow believers. This classic fish eventually became the Jesus fish. The Greek word for fish is ICTHUS. The six letters form an acronym, in Greek, for the acclamation: "Jesus Christ, God's Son, Savior." Some people display the ICTHUS or Jesus fish, hoping that anyone who sees the symbol will substitute the name Jesus for the acronym. You see these symbols everywhere in ecclesiastical art as well as on T-shirts and bumper stickers. I suspect that some Christians sport a "Fish" tattoo. I know a certain Methodist lady whose little blue car is festooned with the fish-like symbol:

Fish are on my mind this May. Not that I do a lot of fishing myself, though the anglers, ever hopeful, migrate by the thousands to Upstate New York's rivers and lakes this time of year. Absent a license to fish, not to mention hook, worm, and sinker, I must depend on the professionals to provide the catch that I fancy on our restaurant menus. As my wife will confirm, I have become a fish fancier in the last seven or eight years, a result, I confess, of the heart attack that I had in 1996. According to that sign posted at Mrs. Faidley's restaurant in Baltimore, eating fish is both helpful to your heart and theologically correct.

Fish rarely appeared on the table in my Iowa youth. The menu at home and especially on my Uncle Charlie's farm, where I spent most of my summers, was heavy on the cholesterol and saturated fats–breakfast, lunch, and supper. Beef and pork were in abundance, with goose at Thanksgiving. Nutritionists today would shudder at the thought of what went down our gullets, year in and year out. Still–Uncle Charlie lived to be over 90. Go figure.

I was envious of my Roman Catholic neighbors who ate fish on Fridays. I am not sure where they got their fish, as northern Iowa is not like Baltimore or Boston, close to ocean. We German Lutherans loved our pork. In the old days, when farmers made their own blood sausage and rinderwurst, it was said that they used every part of the pig except the "oink." Perhaps the day has come when Lutherans, not to mention other non-Roman Catholic Christians, should put fish back on the menu. There is precedent for adopting the fish symbol as our own. Martin Luther the Reformer came up with his own version of the classic marker of a Christian. It is of a fish sticking his tongue out at his Papal persecutors in the 16th-century. The tongue-sticking-out business can be dropped in these days of healthy Protestant-Roman Catholic dialogue, but the notion of non-Roman Catholics eating lots of fish has merit.

The Deer Lake Christian Store in Kalispell, Montana, sells sandals with the message "Jesus Loves You" acting like a giant rubber stamp. For $20.95, you can purchase these "Shoes of the Fisherman" and leave your imprint in the wet sand or soil. It is a novel idea, but I suggest putting your money in a  Missions envelope this May instead. You will be fishing with Jesus just as the early disciples did.

As the miracle of the "loaves and fish" in the Gospel affirms, Jesus was the consummate fisherman. His catch, after all, included you.

June 2013

"Let Us Cross Over the River and Rest"

During the Civil War battle at Chancellorsville, General Robert E. Lee, though victorious, lost nearly a quarter of his army, some thirteen thousand men dead or out of action. The loss of one grieved Lee the most, for Stonewall Jackson was Lee's right arm. Wounded during the battle, Jackson succumbed to pneumonia and on Sunday, May 10, 1863, became so weak that his wife and doctor concluded that he would not last the day. When told of their fears, Jackson rallied and said, "It is all right. It is the Lord's day; my wish is fulfilled. I have always desired to die on Sunday." During the afternoon he dozed off and on, his mind drifting back to the battlefield, and once he called out: "Order A. P. Hill to prepare for action! Pass the infantry to the front . . .. Tell Major Hawks." Then about three p.m. Jackson smiled, closed his eyes, and uttered his last words: "Let us cross over the river and rest under the shade tree."

I remember thinking of the dying Jackson many Junes ago when contemplating our son Matthew's graduation from Cazenovia High School. You might think this strange, except for a character fault I now publicly confess. Some fathers are compulsive smokers, golfers, or football fans. I, however, can be faulted for compulsively planning, especially when it comes to organizing the free time of others. My family constantly complained that I, with calendar in hand, abhor a day, never mind a week, with nothing scheduled. I enjoyed planning a trip as much as the trip itself, and was in my glory on those beautiful sunny summer Saturdays when the whole family was at work--wife hanging out the wash, daughter weeding the strawberries, son mowing the yard, while I washed windows and kept an eye out for any slackers. I was like the dying Stonewall Jackson, ordering A. P. Hill to action and commanding Major Hawks to bring up the reserve troops.

Now you see why I so anticipated June 26, 1994, when Matthew graduated from high school's boot camp. I imagined that he would join the ranks of my small domestic army with an entire summer free. Already I had plans--or should I say, designs on his time. We were to do battle with the house's redwood siding that was in need of sanding and staining, move the firewood to the basement, get him his driver's license, go down to Muhlenberg College where he was to matriculate in the fall, and wage numerous other campaigns, large and small, to make him a better person before I went off to Germany on a year-long Fulbright Fellowship at the end of July.

Does any of this ring true with you, especially those of you who are fathers in this month when we observe Father's Day? I suspect that women, too, can be compulsive doers and organizers, but I have observed that males who grew up in Midwestern farming communities, as I did, are especially prone to the organizer syndrome. Now at age seventy-plus I can no more "fritter away" a summer Saturday watching the Yankees on television than my Uncle Charlie could stay in the house on a rainy day when it was too wet to make hay or harvest oats. He would always find something to do, like splice the hay rope or nail up cow stanchions, and was not content unless my cousin Walter and I left our childish pursuits to clean the tool shed or sweep out the garage.

Perhaps it is time for all of us to come to terms with the Biblical concept of rest, which is more than the absence of busyness. Unrest is a disease of the Soul, a token of the rule of sin (or "vanity" as the Prophet Isaiah wrote) in our lives. It is as dangerous to our emotional, physical, and spiritual health as its opposite--sloth. Proverbs 18:9 says: "He also that is slothful in his work is brother to him that is a great waster." On unrest, the Bible says: "For all his days are sorrows, and his travail grief; yea, his heart taketh not rest in the night. This is also vanity." (Ecclesiastes 2:23) Somehow we have to discover the golden mean between rest and unrest, learn for ourselves, and pass on the lesson.

One of the dangers of authoring these monthly essays is that I am expected to take my own advice. I am not prescribing sloth as the antidote to unrest. Someone, after all, must take out the trash. Some Amazon dwellers were known to simply move their stilted huts when the piles of refuse mound up to the threshold. That's not feasible given American housing. I do prescribe more rest, in the deepest spiritual sense of rest in the Lord as well as rest of the more common sort this summer--an hour in the hammock, twenty minutes with a good book, or an afternoon visiting with friends over iced tea and cookies. Should the voice of dis-ease tempt you, then remember Stonewall Jackson's last words:

"Let us cross over the river and rest under the shade of the trees."

July 2013

An Uplifting Experience!

The mountain man you see at the right is the author at age 40. Brother Gil came to Syracuse in July 1982 to join me in making an ascent of Mt. Marcy in the High Peaks region of the Adirondacks. It was a memorable birthday experience, what with an attack of killer mosquitoes, aching leg muscles, and haphazard meals of our own making (no birthday cake or ice cream). We had planned the climb on the assumption that at age sixty I might not be up to the challenge. Well, my sixtieth, not to mention my seventieth, birthday has come and gone. The shaggy and somewhat fierce climber pictured here holding up an Adirondack trail guide has mellowed some in three decades. A lot of that black hair (what is left anyway) has turned grey.

On my sixtieth birthday in July 2002 (and that of Jan that October), our children and our siblings gave us a certificate for a champagne hot air balloon ride. If you were in the Auburn/Finger Lakes area about sunset on August 1, 2002, and looked to the skies you would have seen the Sernetts floating up, up, and away in the gondola of the Morning Glory. This was a first for us, and I confess to having been nervous, though Jan enjoyed the ride. I am a "feet on the ground" kind of guy. According to the balloonist, the propane-propelled craft met all FAA standards, but I was worried about the answer he gave to a query novice floaters ask. Question: "What happens if a bird flies into a balloon?" Answer: "It would likely bounce off." Why "likely" I wondered; don't balloonists know by now, or does it depend on the size and attitude of the bird?

In telling son Matt (who lives in Seattle) about our "uplifting experience," I observed that at age eighty I will be too old for strenuous activity like mountain climbing and too timid (or wise) to climb into a basket of woven rattan attached to a nylon envelope. By then, I may well have developed an aversion to hot air balloons and think of them much as did those French farmers in the 1700s. Never having seen hot air balloons, the farmers attacked them with pitchforks. Consequently, balloonists began to carry bottles of champagne to mollify the angry public. I said to Matt that I would be satisfied on my 80th birthday for God's angels to carry me away. Somewhat alarmed at this prospect, he suggested that a space ship would do just fine and that I should ask the angels to hold off until I turned one hundred!

Life, like hot air ballooning, has its vicissitudes. In ballooning, the downs are as good as the ups, but, as all of us have experienced from time to time, when you are born into "this mortal coil" (to use a Shakespearean metaphor) there is no guarantee that the ride will always be smooth or the landing uneventful. Bad things happen to good people, a moral conundrum that baffles our innate sense of fair play. If God is in control, then why do the righteous suffer while sinners seem to prosper? The stock market takes a dive, corporate executives who have been cooking their company's books bail out early and pocket millions of dollars. In contrast, ordinary workers see their retirement nest eggs dwindle and the innocent lose faith in the American dream.

Children seem to discover the power (and mystery) of the word "fair" about the third grade, maybe earlier, as was the case with the two little Sernetts--Matthew and Rebecca. "Dad, that's not fair!" is a stinging accusation coming from one's progeny, especially if one thinks of themselves as a reasonably good (and just) parent. Usually a child's use of the concept of fairness at an early age decodes as "I didn't get as much pumpkin pie as my sister," or "Catherine's parents let her go to the movies. Why not me?"

As the decades go by, our sense of fairness matures, more closely approximating the Biblical concept of justice. We pray, "Oh Lord, deal with me not as I deserve, but as you will. Be merciful, and gracious in the name of Jesus. Amen." I turned seventy-one this month (on July 21). Seven decades of personal ups and downs have taught me an important lesson. I do not want God to deal with me fairly, as I deserve. I would be in serious trouble. When our allotted time riding in the gondola called Earth nears an end, and we face the prospect of going before the divine bar of justice, we must plead guilty and fall back to stand in the shadow of the Cross of Christ. From that vantage point, we hope to be lifted up for the final ascent into the arms of the everlasting God.

August 2013

Searching for Love

While scanning the classified section of the Sunday newspaper many years ago, my eye inadvertently fell upon the personal ads placed by singles. I was then attending Faith Lutheran Church up in Cicero. There she was, a "Lutheran Woman, 29, 5' 5''" seeking a "handsome, kind, generous Lutheran Man who has a variety of interests." Knowing myself to be Lutheran and male, I accepted the "handsome, kind, [and] generous" attributes as a matter of fact. And "variety of interests" fitted me perfectly, though I wondered what a woman who enjoys, as the ad stated, "the outdoors, travel, SU, [and] sports" would think of someone who has a collection of toy tractors and makes a sport of riding the lawnmower. I soon discovered that this was all irrelevant, for the ad specified a search for someone between 31 and 36. I was disqualified.

Feeling rejected, I sought consolation in neighboring personals. One had been placed by an "athletic, adventurous" single who liked to roller blade, mountain bike, raft, hike, and dance.   I can do only one of the five. Then there was the "heart out on sleeve, spontaneous Divorced Christian mom" looking for a "nonsmoker, nondrinker, and drug-free" Christian Gentleman, 45-55. The age range was on target, and I scored a near perfect match on her three other criteria. This was becoming interesting. How about the Sicilian Female who promised to treat me like a king? Then I stopped, feeling as if I were prying into the lives of others, an uninvited guest.

What is it about contemporary American culture that makes these personal ads necessary and popular? I understand that many singles have become tired and even fearful of the bar scene. Dating and matchmaking services thrive, and each week's paper promises many new ads in the "Personal Line." In the 19th-century, immigrant German farmers promised marriage to girls from the Old Country, sight unseen, due to the shortage of females on the frontier. Today's "blind date" is a close approximation, and a thirty-word ad in the local newspaper is not far behind. The loss of community and neighborhood, the incessant mobility of job and residence, have contributed to a lack of connectedness. Is there a remedy?

I decided to play "matchmaker" myself and, hoping to help out our Lutheran female, scanned the want ads from men. There was a "winter couch potato" in his late fifties. Nope. Won't do. How about the "energetic biologist" in Fulton or the "rugged farmer" in Watertown seeking someone interested in cows and farming? Problem. Denominational affiliation not specified. I found not a Lutheran in the bunch, and only 2 of the approximately 130 males advertised themselves as Christians. One sought a tall companion. The other declared an interest in a mate who was "kind, gentle, and physically fit." Might do.

Jan and I celebrate 48 years of Christian marriage this month and except for the year I was in Germany as a Fulbright scholar and the nine months or so she was in Baltimore doing health care consulting, we have never been separated. We plan on growing old together, so I have no need to peruse the personals and beg the forgiveness of those good people whose lives I intruded on by reading their all too public displays of loneliness.

My wife and I met in our twenties on a Concordia, St. Paul Lutheran college choir tour. I had my eye on this cute alto for some time, but was a shy guy and only first spoke to her when the two of us teamed up to chase a stray cat out of the sanctuary of a church in Upper Michigan, or was it South Dakota? I think of that cat as providential, a sign from heaven that we two were destined for each other. I shudder to think of what would have happened had I resorted to an ad on the Personal Line. I didn't have much to offer prospective "Mrs. Rights."

Any attempt at humor aside, there is serious business here. Loneliness can weigh heavily on the heart, especially for those who find themselves without a partner to share life's sorrows and joys. Companionship is a precious gift, to be treasured always. But God looks upon all of us--whether we dance the dance of life as single, married, divorced, widower, widow, etc.--in the same way. Some congregations give the impression that they care primarily for families with children--but God welcomes us all the same. No personal ad, however cleverly written, gains us special merit with God.

Of Jesus, the Gospel writer St. Luke says,

"The Son of Man is come to seek and to save that which was lost."

Who's Been Sitting in My Pew?

If you have missed a Sunday or two this past summer, you may find someone else sitting in your favorite pew this September. Church-going regulars who know the rules of the pew may be a bit miffed at being displaced, but shuffling sitting arrangements can be a sign of church growth. New members don't know that the regulars plant themselves in the same spot for so long that their sitters have worn distinctive patterns into those oaken benches.

We are the same people who as children had regular places at the kitchen table. In my case, each of the four Sernett kids not only had a customary place to sit but also our own colored metal glass (formerly holding cottage cheese). Mine was gold.

I thought about congregational seating patterns when visiting St. John's Lutheran Church in rural northern Iowa some years back. As a youngster, I attended Sunday school, VBS, and worship services at St. John's while staying during the summer on my Uncle Charlie's farm. The congregation was an old German one. Curiously, the women and the pre-Confirmation children sat in the nave or main worship area of the church while the old men and young males who had survived the rite of passage that Lutheran Confirmation was, sat up in the balcony. I can still remember the Sunday that my Aunt Elsie allowed my cousin Walt and me to go up there to sit among the adult males, some of whom, I noticed, habitually dozed off once the sermon began.

Ethnic Lutheran rules of the pew might as well have been another set of commandments. The folks at St. John's looked askance at any one who sat where he did not belong. When a cousin of my cousin, a confirmed young male adult with the first name of Carol, dared to sit in the nave with the woman and children, the church gossip mill ground furiously. Carol later became congregational president. He taught my Sunday school class, and I found him to be one of the most knowledgeable of the members at St. John's. Still, tongues wagged.

In the Old Country, among Scandinavian Lutherans in particular, worshippers sat where their family name was rosemaled or inscribed on the ends of the pews. Having someone sit in your pew was as bad as having an interloper sleep in your bed. Though German Lutherans did not always practice the custom of "pew rent" as Cazenovia Methodists did when they built the "Old Stone Church" in 1832, they likewise held to fixed seating patterns, usually demarcating differences in gender and age. However, in America, these hard and fast habits weakened as the immigrants became acculturated. Carol was one of the first truly modern Lutherans at St. John's.

Thinking back on my personal pew habits, I am surprised at how constant they have been. In multiple church settings, from childhood to late middle-age adult, I have generally sat on the right side, about two-thirds of the way back. Once I attended a Lutheran church in the round and felt totally discombobulated. I like the traditional pew setup—with a left side and a right side. I have generally observed the first commandment of pew etiquette. Do not sit in the first two rows, unless forced to do so at Christmas when the church is packed and there is no room but up there. I also tend to avoid the way-way back, as those pews were allocated to mothers with fussy infants before there were "cry rooms."

Somewhere I got the notion that the right side is the liturgically considered the Gospel side, a subtle though wrong-headed assumption that to be on the right is preferable to being on the left. Don't the saints sit at the right hand of God? The left, including the left hand, implies something less than holy, perhaps even sinister. You may remember the days when schoolteachers tied the left arms of children behind their backs to encourage them to write with their right hand. The left-handed have had to endure a kind of second-class citizenship for generations. My mother, who was naturally left-handed but learned in school to write "the correct way," complained of how hard it was to find a left-handed scissor to use when she sewed.

I wonder what the seating arrangements will be in Heaven. Psalm 110:1 reads: "The Lord said unto my Lord, 'Sit thou at my right hand, until I make thine enemies thy footstool.'" Quoted five times in the New Testament, this passage underscores the image of Jesus as "the Right Hand of God." Most Biblical scholars do not interpret this as a positional relationship, as if there were two deities, God the Father and God the Son, with Jesus, the Son sitting at the right hand of the Father. Instead, the image is meant to invoke in us a sense of awe.

Because of His sacrificial death and resurrection, Jesus has conquered all enemies that would separate us from God and now sits Himself on the Throne of Heaven. This pictorial poetry is carried over into the Book of Revelations, where the writer says (Chapter 7, verse 9): "After this I beheld, and, lo, a great multitude, which no man could number, of all nations, and kindreds, and people, and tongues, stood before the throne, and before the Lamb, clothed with white robes, and palms in their hands."

Look closely now with the visionary eyes of one of faith. See yourself in that "great multitude" standing before the heavenly throne giving praise. There are no divisions in that royal assembly, no right and no left. Stand (or sit) where you please.

There is room for all.

October 2013

"His Master's Voice"

When the fall foliage starts to flame, a blanket of nostalgia descends upon our household. I rummage around in closets and turn up an assortment of old things. There is no accounting for such behavior. It is the obverse of spring-cleaning, I suppose.

One fall, I transposed old LPs onto CDs, for I did not have the heart to toss out our collection of vinyl platters begun nearly fifty years ago without preserving the music my wife and I treasure as a chronicle of our lives. So it was that I spent a Saturday morning listening to an old record with the title "His Master's Voice." The singer was George Beverly Shea, better known as "Bev" to his legions of fans.

We had three Shea records, the oldest of which, "Christmas Hymns," dates back to 1959, when Jan and I were beginning our senior years in high school, unaware of each other but apparently predisposed to liking the sound of a deep and velvety bass singing the message of the Good Book.

Bev Shea is not, as I long thought, a good ol' southern boy, though he has long been associated with gospel music and Billy Graham, products of the religious culture of the American South. He was born in Winchester, Ontario, Canada, the son of a Methodist minister. One of the original members of the Graham crusade team and longtime gospel singer on the Graham "the Hour of Decision" radio series, Bev aged before our eyes.

Shea passed away in Asheville, North Carolina, on April 16, 2013, at the remarkable age of 104. Inmates at the Louisiana State Penitentiary had the honor of making the casket in which Shea was buried. Shea visited the prison prior to his death to inspect the handiwork of the inmates. One of them approached Shea, grasped his hand and said in a voice filled with awe, "I have never met a man who is 104." Bev Shea deadpanned, "I haven't either."

For readers who are too young to have heard George Beverly Shea in his prime, I can only say that his voice, so deep and resonant, was the perfect instrument to capture the power of the old hymns he favored. I cannot sing "Nearer My God to Thee" or "Sweet Hour of Prayer" without hearing Bev in my head and wishing God had given me such a voice with which to bring legions of the unrepentant to their knees. It is said that when the Graham crusade went to Australia many years ago, Shea's records outsold rock-and-roll ones during the height of the rock-and-roll craze.

I know that it is the message and not the medium that is important. God uses many means to communicate the truth that "He's Got the Whole World in His Hands." Still each of us wishes that we were more gifted, more eloquent in sharing "The Wonder of It All." In our media-saturated age, where preachers have taken to Power-Point sermons and electronic gadgetry fills the newest temples of the Lord, it is hard to see how Christians gifted with a so-so voice and only a Sunday school knowledge of "What God Has Promised" can be heard through the din of modernity.

"The Wonder of It All," to borrow the title of another of Bev's favorite hymns, is that God does not require us to be gold-plated winners, only gold-plated faithful. When Shea was once asked where he would like to be when Christ returned, he said "On pitch!" Given his musical gifts, Shea might have been a star of stage and screen, but he chose instead to use his talent in the service of the Lord. "I'd Rather Have Jesus," his song says.

We live in a noisy world.

With so much to distract us from being faithful witnesses for Jesus, it is all the more important to listen for the Master's voice. Then "Standing on His Promises," we shall be "Rocked in the Cradle of the Deep."

November 2013

"With Malice Toward None"

The schoolchild in you knows that the Pilgrims first observed Thanksgiving Day in 1621. President Abraham Lincoln made it a national holiday in 1863 at the urging of Sarah Joseph Hale, editor of Godey's Lady's Book. Our country was at the time deeply divided, and Yankee and Reb soldiers, many of them mere boys, lay dying on battlefields with names like Chickamauga and Gettysburg. Skeptics might be forgiven a bit of mockery on the last Thursday of November as Old Abe called the nation to remember God's gracious dealings with the Republic fourscore and seven years old. Presidential proclamations could not blanket the agony of soul felt in thousands of households where an empty chair at the Thanksgiving table signaled the loss of life wrought by mini-balls and battlefield diseases.

When our son Matthew turned 21 in 1997, he was already older than the typical combat soldier in the Civil War or, as far as I know, America's conflicts since then. Compulsory military service has ended, making those Selective Service cards my high school classmates and I carried around for years, artifacts of history. Talk to young males now of the Draft and you get quizzical looks, nothing like the trepidation boys and their families experienced not that long ago. I escaped the Draft when on August 21, 1968, Mary Judy of Franklin County L.B. 13-35, signed and stamped my Selective Service card and classified me as 5-A. Some of my friends were not so fortunate. While I struggled with Greek and Hebrew in divinity school, they fought far costlier battles in places far from home. None of my classmates died in Southeast Asia, but the fifty thousand plus names on the Vietnam Memorial in Washington, D.C., are eloquent and moving testimonials to the personal tragedy of war.

I was moved to contemplate all of this while visiting our nation's capital some years back. I paid my respects to soldiers of my generation who died in Vietnam, and then went round the tidal basin to see the memorial to those who paid the ultimate sacrifice in the Korean conflict. Life-like full body sculptures of soldiers, outfitted in heavy winter gear, slog up a simulated Korean battlefield. Words cannot convey the emotional impact of the moment. I had entered the cathedral of time. The only proper response was prayerful silence.

I am not sure why the memorial to the men and women who died when General Douglas MacArthur tried to force the North Korean army back across the 38th parallel cut to the quick. Perhaps it was because I remember a cousin who was called up from the farm and sent half way round the world to pull dying fighter pilots from their burning planes. He came back to the hog lots and hay fields of the Midwest without serious injury, but something dark lurked within. When flashbacks loosed the demons of memory, my cousin drank to drive them away. In the end the bottle won.

On the forth Thursday of this month, our nation will observe another day of Thanksgiving. Yet we have military personnel stationed beyond our borders. Some of them are in harm's way. Can we reasonably hope that American youth born in 2013 will reach maturity and start families of their own without having to fire a gun in defense of our national interests? Abraham Lincoln understood how terrible war is, even a war fought to preserve the peace, or as he hoped, these United States of America.

Lincoln was a deeply religious man, though not in the conventional sense. He belonged to no Christian church, having been put off by denominational dogma and empty rituals. Wife Mary said of our 16th President--he was "not a technical Christian." Yet Lincoln understood the deeper meaning of the struggle for national unity and the necessity of a national day of Thanksgiving. His Second Inaugural Address gives voice to how precious a gift peace is and how strongly we must hold on to it by choosing love over hatred.

With malice toward none; With charity for all;
With firmness in the right, as God gives us to see the right,
Let us strive on to finish the work we are in;
To bind up the nation's wounds;
To care for him who shall have borne the battle,
And for his widow, And his orphan--
To do all which may achieve and cherish
a just and lasting peace among ourselves,
And with all nations.

Abraham Lincoln, March 4, 1865

December 2013

How to Avoid Eileschpijjel's Christmas

The Pennsylvania Dutch tell stories ("noodle tales") of a beloved character known as Eileschpijjel. He is a trickster spirit. Folktales about Eileschpijjel are as old as German myths and legends of the 13th-century. They are rooted in north European jokes about a not-too-bright but well-meaning peasant whose habit is doing things in his own peculiar way. According to one story, Eileschpijjel needed wood one winter and went to gather it in the forest with a two-horse team. As he threw piece after piece on the wagon he said, "If the horses can pull this piece, they can pull the next one." And so he piled the wagon high. Then he found that the horses couldn't pull the load. Eileschpijjel's solution was to unload, throwing piece after piece off, while saying, "If they can't pull this piece, they can't pull the next one." Reasoning thus, he kept on unloading until the wagon was empty. Then he drove home with an empty wagon.

I had an Eileschpijjel-like Christmas once and have regretted it ever since. By the age of twelve or thirteen, I had long given up the notion that Santa Claus visited each child's home on Christmas Eve with a sack full of goodies. I knew where Mother hid the wrapped gifts behind the clothes in the spare closet, and I had seen several packages with my name on them under her bed. Unable to endure the long wait until Christmas, I began to badger and cajole her to allow me to open one gift a day, beginning with those from distant uncles and aunts. I argued that this would give me plenty of time to compose thank you notes and get them out during the holidays. Mother relented and thus day-by-day I opened one gift after another.

Christmas Eve came. We all trooped over to church and then, as was the Sernett custom, returned home to distribute the treasures that had magically appeared under the Christmas tree. I have forgotten who played Santa Claus that year, but when my portion was distributed, the gifts made a very small pile. We opened gifts by going around the family circle, and after a half dozen cycles or so, I had nothing left. And so I sat there glumly looking on, as my brother and sisters, who had not badgered and cajoled, continued the rounds.

The Christmas and holiday season is soon upon us, and we shall once again busy ourselves with a thousand and one things. Like Eileschpijjel, we want more than is our capacity to carry. Many Americans will ring up huge totals on their charge cards these next few weeks, postponing payment to next year. Others rush here and there, complaining of the hassle of getting ready for the big day. Frequently our expectations of the "perfect" Christmas fail to materialize, and we move wearily into the New Year. It's time to stop adding burden upon burden to our Christmas wagon.

I am not sure that Eileschpijjel's method of reasoning is the answer to our dilemma. If we strip away all of those activities that make the holiday season special, we end up with Eileschpijjel's empty wagon--days no different than the dead of winter in February. Thus I look forward to the hustle and bustle-- putting up the tree, getting the decorations out of the basement, Christmas cookies, caroling, cards from friends and relatives, and, of course, the Christmas eve candlelight service. That puts everything else into perspective, balancing out the wagonload of our holiday experience. There is something beyond words in that moment when the candles are lit, we sing Silent Night, receive the Christmas benediction and walk out into the night with home as our destination.

I learned an important lesson as a result of that Christmas of the Great Disappointment when I opened most of my gifts before Christmas Eve. Part of the joy of this special season is in the anticipation and expectation of what is yet to come. This, of course, is the meaning and purpose of Advent. The Church's liturgical calendar includes four Sundays in the Christmas Cycle prior to our celebration of the Nativity of our Lord. There was a time when I thought this too much for the young to bear. And so I secretly prayed that God would fast forward Advent. After all, I reasoned, we all knew how the Christmas story turned out. Why not jump right to the big event? What was the point of four long weeks of waiting for it?

Now much older, and, I hope, a little wiser, I think that I understand. We must wait because we must prepare. That was the message of John the Baptist who went about announcing the coming of the Redeemer King.

On Jordan's banks the Baptist's cry
Announces that the Lord is nigh;
Awake and hearken, for he brings
Glad tidings of the King of kings!

Then cleansed be ev'ry life from sin;
Make straight the way for God with-in,
And let us all our hearts prepare
For Christ to come and enter there.

January 2014

Free and Clear!

When mortgage rates nosedived years ago, I got ours out and thought of going for one of those refinancing plans. My wife and I are homeowners in name only, as the bank held a piece of paper which gives it the right to claim our house and property should we default on the loan we took out. Like many others tempted by falling interest rates, we liked the idea of cheap money. Fortunately, we resisted. Refinancing would only stretch out the bank's lien on our life. I have heard those television pitchmen say that you can build wealth by borrowing money and investing it in real estate, and I know about the so-called tax advantages of a home mortgage or home equity loan.

In the old days (that is any year prior to 1960 when I graduated from high school), folks thought poorly of being chained to a mortgage. Churches celebrated when the last payment was made with a liturgical burning–the president of the congregation torched the document to symbolize redemption from the moneylenders. Neighbors yearned to make that last payment on their property before they retired. When they did, you could tell it by the

114

bounce in their step. When rumors went round that some hardworking farmer had died and left his heirs under the curse of monthly payments to secure their legacy, the judgment was made, fair or not, that the farmer had been a failure. To go into the next world, free of debt, that was our goal.

The start of a new year is a good time for Christians to check their personal balance sheets. What or who has a lien on your soul? Sometimes the forces that tie us down are of our own doing; sometimes they come at us through no fault of our own. I find it hard to empathize with Christians who complain of their lot in life while at the same time indulging in habits known to be detrimental to the welfare of body and soul. They are no wiser than the homeowners who, piling mortgage upon mortgage, wake up one day to discover that they have no equity left, nothing to call their own. I have much more empathy for the Christians who struggle heroically against pain and suffering of the kind that can blind side us through no fault of our own. It is in their struggling with the question "Oh, God, why Me?" that I am instructed in the fundamentals of prayer, and piety, and hope.

By now some of you reading these thoughts will have detected a flaw in my analogy. Wrestling with the demons that plague a Christian's life is not exactly like living with a mortgage on your house. In the latter case, one always has the option to sell out and move on, maybe downsizing in the process or, horror of horrors, going back to renting or living with the relatives. Can we really move on so easily? My wife and I have tested the idea, and we have discovered that the first and most difficult problem is to find some other place we would both rather be. Try the test for yourself. Go to www.findyourspot.com on the Internet and answer the questions in the nine or so panels. You will have many choices to make, such as whether or not you prefer ocean surfing to skiing, hunting or the symphony, Methodists or Lutherans, small towns or big. Then click the findyourspot search button and see what turns up. If you are braver (have more faith) than Jan and I, make a pledge (write it out) that you will move/retire to the top pick before the results display. I hope you have better luck than we did.

Number 1 on my list of 24 "top spots" was—yes, hold the drum roll, Branson, Missouri, which is touted as having more live shows and theater seats than Broadway or Las Vegas. I was devastated. I have not been to a "live show" on Broadway for a quarter century, and I'm no more likely to move to Las Vegas than I am to Baghdad. There are a couple of intriguing spots on my list: New Harmony, Indiana, site of an 1814 Utopian planned community; Berea, Kentucky, said to have the highest concentration of Tibetans in the country (Why Tibetans in Berea?); Spencer, Iowa, with its annual "Thanks for Franks" parade, featuring over 60 purveyors of hot dogs; Hannibal, Missouri, home of Huck Finn and Tom Sawyer; and Boone, North Carolina, host of the Firefly Folk Festival each summer. Jan looked at my list and complained that the towns were all too small, especially Arrow Rock, Missouri, which boasts a population of 70. I pointed out to her that if we moved to Arrow Rock it would have a population of 72.

Jan's list of "top spots" began with Fargo, North Dakota. I wonder if Jan remembers the movie? Other cities on her list were Spokane, Minneapolis-St. Paul, Duluth, Des Moines, Bangor, Kalamazoo, and Syracuse! Yes, Syracuse, New York, where we lived from 1975-1990, until moving out to Madison County. What could this mean? Is she the contented one and I the restless soul? Are we destined to go our separate ways, she to a city with concerts and commerce and I to a small hamlet or bend in the road with cows and corn?

Perhaps the benefit of the findyourspot.com exercise, apart from the diversion from winter worries it offers, is the discovery that true contentment comes thru dealing with whatever circumstances you find yourself in, armed with informed faith. Just as you sign a mortgage only after reading the fine print, so you should enter into 2014 fully aware of your spiritual balance sheet. In doing this self-exam, you will be directed once again to the bottom line–the core Christian narrative:

God in Christ Jesus has satisfied our debt. The mortgage chaining us to sin and death is no more.

We have a permanent shelter in the heart of God. Rejoice!

Taking Inventory

I dreamt of Martha the other night, thought it strange, and rummaged through my mind for the symbolic meaning of it all. Martha died in 1914 at the Cincinnati zoo, mourned by few except the custodians of Mother Nature's family. Perhaps the angels shed a

tear too. With her death, Martha joined company with the Carolina Parakeet, the Great Auk, and the Steller's Sea Cow, all extinct. Martha, you see, was the very last Passenger Pigeon. Last seen in the wild in 1889, Passenger Pigeons once numbered in the millions but were slaughtered wholesale until only Martha was left to represent God's handiwork. Then she too died, leaving a hole in creation.

Though dream psychology, like talk of alien space invaders, amuses rather than enlightens me, I did consult Plough's Birthday and Dream Book, a curiosity found among my mother's personal effects after her death. Plough (manufacturer of beauty products in the 1920s and 1930s) believed that a pigeon in a dream means "wealthy marriage soon." I thought this ridiculous, since no one consulted my wife of nearly fifty years. Had I dreamt of a quail ("Good Omen"), a turkey ("Gain in business"), an owl ("Admiration"), or even a Jay Bird ("Visit from friends"), I might have been prepared to believe Plough, but Martha was clearly a pigeon.

So I set aside the dream book and reflected once more on the Passenger Pigeon. In the inventory of God's world, did the demise of Martha cause concern? The Bible is silent regarding the passenger pigeon, though doves and eagles abound. What difference did it make, that the passenger pigeon had once been and now is no more? When I pass from the earth (not in the Cincinnati zoo, I hope), will those who make the inventory of significant events take any notice? Will I have made enough of a mark on the world's conscience so that I will be missed? Such a jumble of February musings! I felt a spiritual kingship with the character played by the actor Jimmy Stewart in the old movie, "It's a Wonderful Life." He thought his rather humdrum and ordinary life was small potatoes on the table of life, ruled as it is by the rich and powerful.

February is a good month for personal stocktaking. You may feel that the treadmill of daily cares has worn you down to the point where you do not make a difference. You cannot resign from life, but you'd like to. When the icy fingers of depression grip your heart, then think of these things. You are beloved of God. Like Martha, you are a very special creation--unique and irreplaceable. You may not be able to fly with eagles or coo like a dove, but you do have a place in the divine aviary. I have a banner in my study, made by a student at the seminary where I once taught. The hand of God, pointer finger extended, directs one's eye to the following text: "Milton, I have called you by name; you are mine." Isaiah 43:1 You should, of course, insert your own Christian name, thereby reminding yourself that in God's inventory you have a place reserved for all time.

I enjoy looking at old photographs, particularly those of family reunions, church picnics, city scenes, or any picture of crowds from a century ago. Rarely do I recognize an individual, so I try to reconstruct something of the lives of those whom history has forgotten. Like those you love and care for, these strangers laughed and cried, making the best they could of what life gave them. I suspect a percentage of them were crooks and scoundrels, maybe worse, but in the faces staring back at me, I see something of myself, family, friends, and neighbors. None of us has ever made Who's Who in America, yet collectively we belong to a segment of the tapestry of life without which the world would be the poorer. Pull on the thread representing just one individual and all others are weakened.

While in high school I worked at Harrison's Dime Store in Hampton, Iowa, and remember well the day early in the new year when we shut the doors to do inventory. At first counting everything one by one was enjoyable; by late afternoon tedium set in, and we would resort to counting the smaller things wholesale rather than individually. Thank goodness that the Lord does not weary of us. God knows us by name. When Jesus sent his disciples out to preach and perform miracles, he encouraged them by telling them: "The very hairs of your head are all numbered." (Matthew 10: 30)

In the same chapter of Matthew's Gospel, Jesus tells the disciples that not one sparrow can fall to the ground without God noticing. This passage has troubled me over the years; I have been the agent of many a sparrow's death, indirectly, at least. On Uncle Charlie's farm, the sparrows that nested under the eves of the garage, chicken house, and other outbuildings were thought of as enemies. They stole corn and other grain. So at least once a summer, my cousin Walter and I armed ourselves with long sticks and poked baby sparrows from their homes. Some fell to the ground, a treat for the cats. Others we disposed of in the horse tank--to see if they could swim, I guess. I should have asked our Sunday School teacher there at the country Lutheran church in northern Iowa why God would be concerned about sparrows when they, like the crows in the cornfield, were dead set against our welfare.

I suspect that the answer lies in the observation that in the divine inventory of things, God cares for us all the more because even the lowly sparrow is not forgotten. Unlike the Passenger Pigeon, the common sparrow is unlikely ever to become extinct. Thus each time you look upon one, think how much more you are beloved of God and important to all around you.

March 2014

Pure Christianity & New York Grade A Light Amber

Warm days and cool nights in March signal the arrival of "sugaring off" season in New York State. Neighbor Brisbane to the north of us winters in Florida and twenty years ago or so offered to turn his entire maple syrup making operation over to yours truly. There were over fifty acres of trees, a sugarhouse the size of a vacation cottage, an evaporator that appeared to be partially disassembled, gathering tanks, buckets, metal spigots, and assorted other paraphernalia. My maple syrup making skills were and still are those of a rank amateur.

I talked with several members of the New York State Maple Producers Association seeking counsel in the art of transforming sap to syrup and came away with the impression that what may be a winter diversion to me is a religion to others. Old-timers swear by their secret rituals and tell of attending to the boiling liquid in the evaporator as if it were the elixir of eternal life. They think nothing of staying up all night when the sap is boiling. As the column of steam rises above the sugar shack and the entire surface of the boiling pan tosses and turns, the devotees wait for just the right moment to draw off the syrup. Skilled maple producers attend to every detail with the dedication of monks at a holy shrine. Their ultimate goal is high quality Grade A syrup, which can contain no less than 66 percent sugar. New York Grade A Light Amber--the lightest of the three classifications in taste and color--is the Holy Grail.

A bottle of "Log Cabin" sits in our refrigerator, bought at Wegmans as I recall. It is but 2% real maple syrup. Some grocery store products contain less than that. When I offered the real thing--New York Grade A Light Amber--to a house guest recently, I was informed that he preferred the artificial stuff. He thought pure maple syrup tasted funny, as if it were the imposter. What a peculiar turn-of-events! What would William Burt, founder of the Leader Evaporator Company in 1888 in Vermont and pioneer in introducing the first flue type evaporator to the industry, think? He would surely be saddened by our preference for cheap substitutes, just as Moses was when he came down from Mt. Sinai and discovered that the Israelites had fashioned a Golden Calf to worship [Exodus 32].

I refrain from becoming too self-righteous, for the butter we use is not real butter, the milk we drink is skim milk, and I once ate a soy burger. Nevertheless, I maintain that holding on to the authentic in life is worth the struggle. There is no substitute for the unadulterated Gospel. An imitation Christ is an icon without power. Authentic Christianity is something worth preserving in an age where being a Christian means little more to many people than wearing the label. The apostolic Church defined pure Christianity as "the Gospel of Jesus Christ, the Son of God." [Mark 1.1] When St. Paul wrote to those calling themselves Christians in Galatia, he warned them about accepting any other gospel than what he had preached--"Justification by Faith in Christ Jesus." One of the hallmarks of the authentic Christianity is that we hold to the Gospel as absolutely genuine--"all wool and a yard wide."

In Amateur Sugar Maker, Noel Perrin describes how before 1800 New Englanders got sap out of a maple. The early settlers simply went to their sugar orchards with sharp axe in hand. They would give each tree a good whack, sap would trickle down the bark, and a hollowed-out piece of pine log served as a gathering bucket. "The great flaw to the system," Perrin writes, " was that it usually killed the trees within five years. Maples don't like being whacked." Today the art of maple sugaring is far more complex, not to mention expensive, if one is just starting out. As Perrin says, "when you're producing a sacred article, you don't have to maximize your cash return." If you are out and about on the country roads this March and April, you will see signs such as "Pure Maple Syrup Sold Here." A gallon may cost you as much as sending a family of four to the movies. Pay the farmer with a smile. His profit margin is close to zero when time and labor are factored in. His rewards are almost entirely intrinsic--the taste of real maple syrup on a stack of buckwheat pancakes and the satisfaction of accepting no substitutes.

The Leader Evaporator Co., Inc., of St. Albans, Vermont, is one of the oldest such firms in the country. It boasts that it has been in "Continuous Service Since 1888." This is quite a claim, given the fact that in some seasons the sap has been exceedingly thin. Despite our ups and downs, the good folks at Cazenovia's Methodist Church can proudly advertise--"Continuous Service Since 1832" and the folks at the Nelson Methodist Church can claim "Continuous Service Since 1833."

April 2014

Easter's Musical Olympics

Church musicians live for Easter. It is their Olympic decathlon, their last game of the World Series, their Indianapolis 500. During the rest of the liturgical year, perhaps with the exception of Christmas (when they are often upstaged by tiny tots and towering trees of green), they slog along in the trenches of anonymity and ingratitude. We pew sitters take it for granted that each Sunday's service will have an accompanist, a term denoting secondary fiddle status to some people.

We are wrong, of course, but then we are thickheaded and do not appreciate the wonderful musical heritage left us by Christian composers. Too easily satisfied with the musical mush blared at us on contemporary radio and television stations, we look on in puzzlement when someone tells us that listening to Johann Sebastian Bach's B-minor Mass is too profoundly moving to be expressed in words.

I am among the musically challenged for whom the virtues of Bach's B-minor mass remain a mystery. My budding career as a piano prodigy was cut short because of a dog. I took lessons from Mrs. Wilson back there in Iowa. Whenever she went off to answer the phone in the kitchen, the family dog, a black Cocker Spaniel, would rush into the living room and bite my feet. I complained to my mother who allowed me to quit (probably sensing that my keyboard talents were limited anyway). Later I played B-flat clarinet in Hampton High School Band. I was good at scales, lousy at timing. Mr. Feeze, our band director, caught on that I was leaning on others. Unable to count those long rests, I would start to play only after I had seen other second clarinets do so. Consequently, I came in a split second behind every one else. Feeze detected the same laggardness in marching band and once pointedly told me, "Get with it, Sernett." This hurt, but then the fault may have been in my genes. No one ever called we four Sernett children "musically gifted." You should hear my sister sing.

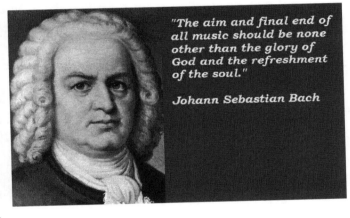

"The aim and final end of all music should be none other than the glory of God and the refreshment of the soul."

Johann Sebastian Bach

The Bach family of central Germany was a musical dynasty. It began with the baker Viet Bach (d. 1619) who delighted in playing the cittern (a kind of lute) while his grist mill was grinding. This, according to Johann Sebastian, his most famous descendent, "taught him to keep time." Among the forbearers of the architect of the Mass in B minor were town musicians, organists, composers, conductors, and, to add variety to an otherwise phenomenally musical family, several highly successful painters. Johann Sebastian was born in 1685 in central Germany at Eisenach, known in all Protestant countries as the city of Luther. Bach's father, Johann Ambrosius, was town musician, and an uncle, Johann Christoph, was an organist.

Bach's road to musical greatness is too complex to relate here, though it is instructive to note that his life was not without trouble and sorrow. Both parents died by the time he was ten, jealous rivals harped on him, his first wife expired while he was away on a trip, and seven of the thirteen children of his second wife did not survive infancy. Once Bach was thrown into jail for "too obstinately requesting his dismissal" from the court of Anhalt-Cöthen. Even at Leipzig, where Bach spent his most productive years (1723-1750) and where he was responsible for all of the music in the city's Protestant churches, all did not go well. Bach described the city fathers as "strange people with small love of music" who forced him to "live under almost constant vexation, jealousy, and persecution."

Perhaps the musically gifted in today's world are tempted to echo Bach's remark about "strange people with small love of music." I for one am willing to learn and so once obtained a copy of Bach's B-minor Mass. It is a monumental work of four sections, including the poignant *Crucifixus,* a set of thirteen variations on the same bass line, and the majestic *Credo.* "The colossal dimensions of the Mass," said one musical authority "makes it unsuitable for church services. It belongs to the concert hall, which under the impact of its awe-inspiring majesty turns into a church serving all human beings responsive to religious experience." Another source says, "Certainly the work is liturgically inappropriate for service use."

How about Bach's St. Matthew's Passion as an alternative? It has been called "the climax of Bach's music for the Protestant church," radiating tenderness and love. We only need two mixed choruses (including soloists), two orchestras, and a group of boy singers. This how the hymn tune in the first chorus ought to sound: "Two wildly excited groups confront each other with terse questions and sorrowful answers, against a background of tears suggested by the heaving and milling orchestra. Above this depiction of humanity's passionate grief rises a crystal-clear, serene, church tune, setting the stage for a discourse on mortal frailty and divine strength. Superb artistry is revealed in the employment of the chorale melodies."

Easter Sunday at the Cazenovia and Nelson Methodist churches. I can hear the music now.

Fine. Deo Gloria
("The end. Glory to God")

May 2014

In Memorium

The month of May holds two strong memories for me. School let out in Iowa as Memorial Day approached. When I was young, this meant no more teachers' rules and homework until after Labor Day. For those of us in the High School Band, May was also the month to march out to the Hampton Cemetery where the community held a brief ceremony to honor local residents who had given their lives in de-

fense of our country. We donned our uniforms and white buck shoes for one last time, fell in line behind the flag bearers, played a few patriotic tunes, and, despite Mr. Feeze's orders, broke rank to scramble after the shell casings that flew about when the honor guard fired a salute over the cemetery pond.

I have participated in Memorial Day observances in New England and in Upstate New York, and have observed how common and comfortable the rituals are. Scholars of American religion tell us that Memorial Day, like July 4th, is a hallmark of our national civil religion, a ritual that transcends denominational and sectarian differences and instructs us about being "Americans." Choose your community, especially in small town America, and I will show you bands marching, preachers praying, politicians orating, and flags flying. As a boy of 14, I enjoyed Hampton's effort to create a collective feeling of respect and reverence for those who went off to fight on some foreign field and never returned. I liked the sound and fury of it all, the display of color, and, yes, the theater. The sight of W. W. I veterans, fewer with each passing year, raising bony hands to salute the flag touched me, while the recollection of W. W. II veterans stuffing themselves into uniforms that no longer fit still brings a smile.

The Memorial Days of my youth were usually sunny and bright. School was out, and we marched along in a grand almost giddy manner. We were, after all, young and immortal. We clarinets had the tricky passages of John Philip Sousa's marches down pat. We had nothing to fear as we entered the cemetery gates and wound our way up to the knoll where carpenters had erected a wooden platform the previous night. A half hour later our mood had changed, at least mine usually did. It has taken me some time to understand this transformation. Only recently have I located the source of my discomfort. She always sat in the shadow of the male politicians, military officers, and preachers. She had no role to play in the festivities until it came time to present her with a folded United States flag. She was called "The Gold Star Mother."

In those years a "Gold Star Mother" was a local woman whom the authorities had selected to honor because she had lost a son in one of the World Wars or the Korean War. We had no "Gold Star Fathers," though I am sure that fathers grieved just as much as mothers over the death of those to whom they had given life. Perhaps because men made wars, they felt it necessary to give women this small part in Memorial Day observances.

Now that my mother lays at rest not far from the knoll where we honored Hampton's "Gold Star Mothers," I can understand why I usually left the cemetery with some thing gnawing at my youthful spirits. I was not yet of draft age, but had I been the Selective Service Bureau might have called my number and sent me off to a place of death, and mother would have had no recourse but to watch, and wait, and then weep--just as the "Gold Star Mothers" did. What does the month of May mean to a "Gold Star Mother? How do you reconcile for her Mother's Day and Memorial Day?

All of this came home to me when I was far away from home visiting the Scottish National War Memorial in Edinburgh Castle, Scotland. Opened by the Prince of Wales in 1927, the War Memorial was designed to honor the laddies who died during the Great War of 1914-18. Like most tourists, we were pressed for time, so I could only page through the memorial books that listed each Scottish soldier, his place of birth and place of death. From Scotland's farms and villages, young men went off to die, often in places they and their parents had never heard of. I knew none of the names inscribed in this book of the dead, yet I felt that same tug at the heart I had known when leaving the cemetery after Hampton's Memorial Day many years ago. "The Gold Star Mother" is a universal figure. A Scottish mother and an American mother on Memorial Day walk the cemetery in need of no cultural translator. When they cry, they cry a universal language.

Neither Memorial Day nor Mother's Day are church festivals. We have no rituals, no readings, no theologies specific to May's special days. The great theologians wrote and preached a "Theology of the Cross," not a "Theology of Glory." Every "Gold Star Mother" reminds us to temper the rhetoric of glory that puffs up a nation, making war seem sane. There are no good wars, no good deaths--save one. The "Theology of the Cross" teaches us that if we are to glory, we do so not in "the might of arms" but in Him who wore a Crown of Thorns, in Christ Jesus, the King of Kings who died on a cross.

June 2014

"Dominus Baseball"

Of late I have been meditating on the sport of theology. Much has been said of the theology of sport; essayists have extracted the last ounce of blood from that allegorical goose. Enough of erudite treatises on sport rituals and baseball as the national religion. Is it not time for serious consideration of the sport of theology? A passage from August Derleth's Village Year, subtitled "A Sac Prairie Journal," caught my eye.

Derleth's observations of daily life in Sac Prairie (Sauk City, Wisconsin), first published in 1941, aren't read much these days. I stumbled upon them in a used book store. Originally kept as a private journal, Derleth's record contains some startlingly sharp revelations concerning the connection between theology and sport. The entry for 5 October reads:

I heard today that young David Bachhuber, having a boil on each leg, is positive they come from kneeling too much at Mass. He avers that the priest says during the service, "Dominus baseball," and "Calling all cars!"--this is his interpretation of the Latin he does not understand.

127

Most Protestants dispensed with Latin a long time ago but there is much that we don't understand, really understand, in our liturgy. There is a mystery there.

Our family made a pilgrimage to Cooperstown over in Otsego County when the children were younger. Though we were within a two base hit of the National Baseball Hall of Fame and parked about fifty feet from Abner Doubleday Field, baseball's Holy of Holies, I could not convince Matthew or Rebecca to visit these shrines. They were more fascinated by the Cardiff Giant at Cooperstown's Farm Museum. Having grown up as a fan of the old Brooklyn Dodgers and schooled in the myth that Baseball is the most American of sports, akin to a national religion, I wondered where my efforts at parental modeling had gone wrong. Then a few years later Rebecca salved my guilt by becoming a New York Mets fan.

Few of us at the Cazenovia and Nelson Methodist churches can complain of boils from too frequent kneeling, but we may on occasion feel as if our pastors were saying "Dominus baseball" or "Calling all cars!" Maybe they should on some Sundays when the fog of inattentiveness has spread across the congregation. I take comfort in the sameness of Christian worship, but I also know that familiarity can breed sloth and, in advanced cases, downright bad theology. In the same excerpt from Derleth's chronicle of life in Sauk City, we read:

However, Teddy Williams' break remains to me the most classic. Seen one day gazing intently at a crucifix in church, he was asked by the priest what Christ died of. Without hesitation, Teddy replied: "From eating too much sweet corn."

Young Teddy's problem may have been more than the Latin Mass. Gross inattentiveness, perhaps.

Would the Teddy Williams in all of us pay greater attention if Sunday worship had the suspense of a great sport contest? Would we hang on the preacher's every word if we were in the bottom of the ninth inning of the World Series of Worship, with our souls' fate, our salvation, yet undecided? I suspect we might, but then again I'm not sure we would want to go through the spiritual agony.

The cosmic conflict between Good and Evil has been decided. Christ is the Victor (*Christus Victor*). Hallelujah!! We need not wait until the last inning of our lives to know that in the victorious Christ we too are winners. I can think of nothing more boring than having to watch a replay tape of a baseball game, the outcome of which is in the morning paper. A fan's vested interest in a baseball game ends when the bats are bagged. Your and my interest in the familiar story told each and every Sunday is of a higher order than that of the sport enthusiast.

CHRISTUS VICTOR

When the funeral bell tolls for the Christian, it rings no surprises. Give thanks then for the same old story and make sure you have your season tickets. You'll find me in Seat 7, Row 21, Section 42. Those numbers correspond, by the way, to the month, day, and year of my Baptism. You too have a reserved seat.

July 2014

The Way Home

If the pundits of automobile culture are correct, our cars are extensions of our personalities. My son's Mazda 323 once boasted bumper stickers that read "Land Pirate," "Troll in Trunk "and" Hero for Hire--Tyrants Trashed, Dragons Slain, Maidens Rescued." When he left for London for a semester of study abroad, I drove the Mazda back and forth to the university. As it would not do for a happily married professor to have a sticker telling the world "My

Girlfriend Said She'd Leave Me If I Didn't Give up Gaming. I'm Sure Gonna Miss Her," I thought of removing it and any others my son allowed.

Last month Milly Canestrare, a friend from Faith Lutheran Church, Cicero, passed away. We once were members up at Faith. Milly's death brought to mind this story. One Sunday years ago we were driving out of the parking lot after the second service at Faith when I noticed that Milly's car sported a yellow Smiley on its antenna. That was appropriate. I knew Milly to be an infectiously happy person, all the more so when you got her talking about growing up in the Belvidere/Rockford area of northern Illinois in the years when Lutheran youth still attended barn dances. Milly used the Smiley on her car's antenna so that she could find her vehicle in crowded parking lots.

Edna Rosenwinkel, my wife's mother, was to pick us up at Chicago's O'Hara airport. Our flight was on time, our luggage arrived in good order, and all was going smoothly until we exited the terminal into the parking lot. Acres and acres of cars. Mom Rosenwinkel led the way. We walked and walked and walked. I soon realized that Jan's mother had forgotten where she had parked her Dodge Omni. All cars began to look alike, and our suitcases got heavier by the half-hour. Exhausted herself, Mom "R" had to acknowledge the sad truth--her car was lost. At that moment I would have given $100 for a Smiley face.

I have often wondered how it feels to be lost--I mean really lost. As a child I must have wandered away from my parents on those busy Friday evenings when the Hampton, Iowa, stores stayed open 'til 9 p.m. and the farmers crowded into town, but I don't recall having been frightened. I have taken the wrong fork in the road on many occasions, but by trial and error I have managed to find my way home thus far in life.

I do know the feeling of loss. Once when Matthew was a toddler, he got away from us in K-Mart, and we had to resort to having a "lost child" announcement made. For a brief time, my wife and I experienced the anxiety parents know whose children show up on those missing child posters. Then, there he was by the "blue light special" cart. As I enfolded him in my arms, I thanked Matt's guardian angel for having kept tabs on the little rascal. Matthew didn't appear to be the least bit worried and to this day lives by the philosophy that one can never get truly lost. By going in one direction long enough, Matt says, you are bound to get to something! He also believes that by making three right turns you always end up where you began.

Tell that to the Wisconsin woman who has been lost at least seven times since last September. The press has dubbed Kelli Elias, 39, "the chronically lost hiker." Delafield, Wisconsin, authorities want to bill her for the $2,300 it has cost the town for the park rangers, sheriff's deputies and firefighters who must be sent out each time she uses her cell phone to call 911 and asks to be rescued. Perhaps what Ms. Elias has discovered is the psychological reward of being found. The old-time revivalist preachers knew that in any crowd of potential converts there were repeaters, folks who so enjoyed the emotional high of being saved that they came night after night to answer the altar call.

As baptized members of the Body of Christ, we are part of the divine global positioning system. At every moment and at every place, we are held secure in the arms of God, though by all appearances we seem to have wandered far from the fold and feel that no one will ever answer our cry for help. The Good Shepherd knows us by name, and should we fall into the pit of despair, comes to rescue us and brings us home.

Now unto Him who brought His people forth
Out of the wilderness, by day a cloud,
By night a pillar of fire; to Him alone,
Look we at last and to no other look we.
Stephen Phillips, 1868-1915

August 2014

Smile! You're on God's Time

Researchers now tell us that men have biological clocks too. I know I do, and it is ticking loudly. Every time I pass by a small child with a captivating smile, I pause to think about how old I am, how old our two children are, and what my chances are of seeing our two grandchildren graduate from high school. To put it bluntly, I'm smitten with babies with no hair and big smiles. It must be something hormonal. One day my wife and I were strolling in a local mall when we passed this cute infant with a round head and big smile, making her/him (Who can tell at that age?) look exactly like a smiley face.

You have all seen that ubiquitous graphic, the most iconic version of which was designed by commercial artist Harvey Ball in 1963 as a marketing tool for an insurance company. Smiley faces are everywhere now, even on the national highways you are traveling this August. Some astute construction engineer decided to post smiley face signs along congested roads to dampen down road rage.

There is something about a baby's smile that tames the angry beast in all of us. I have watched the grumpiest of adults be transformed into happy folks at the mere sight of a small child with a big grin and sparkling eyes. I think all of us started out as smiling infants; somewhere along the way, adults lose the gift of the instinctive and innocent smile. While reflecting on my chances of seeing our grandchildren, Amanda and Wade, become young adults, I came upon this weighty theological question. How do babies learn to smile? Is there such a thing as a neonatal smile? Did I smile (say at hearing the sound of a John Deere tractor on my Uncle's farm) while I was yet in the womb?

I asked my wife (who has had more firsthand experience with things neonatal than this writer) how babies learn to smile. Her response was that they learn from their parents. But how? Perhaps infants are merely imitating those smiling heads that hover over their cribs and talk baby talk, cooing like so many turtledoves. If this imitation is the means, could we teach a baby to never smile by never smiling at them? Cultural anthropologists have debated the nurture vs. nature question for decades without arriving at consensus, though we seem to be in an age where all of human behavior is seen as rooted in genetic and biochemical factors. So, is there a DNA code for the smile, a specific gene that some people have more in abundance than others? If human behavior is fundamentally biochemical, then could pharmaceutical companies concoct a happiness pill, so that every one of us would become a joy germ? I know a few people for whom I would prescribe the smiley pill.

Puzzled by all of this, I turned to my Bible. To my surprise, there are no smiles in the Bible, at least if I am to trust the concordance to <u>The New Chain Reference Bible</u> (KJV) that I use. I was at a loss to explain this—no smiles in the Old Testament (but lots of smiting) and no smiles in the New Testament, where one would expect lots of smiles, given the happy events the early Christians experienced. Check it out. One finds no smiles even in the Easter account. The word happy is used in the Bible, as in Proverbs 3:13, "Happy is the man that findeth wisdom, and the man that getteth understanding," and Psalm 144:15, "Happy is that people, whose God is the Lord."

My Hebrew is rusty, and my Greek New Testament is packed away in a box in the barn, so I cannot tell you whether linguistic equivalents existed in the Biblical languages for the word "smile." If they did, it is surely strange that the word escaped the compilers of my concordance. It is too far fetched to speculate that humans did not smile at all in ancient times but used some other form of nonverbal communication to express happiness. What? Wiggle their big toes?

Traditional African languages had no word for "religion." Why? Because primal cultures drew no distinction between the sacred and the secular—everything had religious significance. A society only needs the word "religion" if there is something to set it against, like the profane (from the Latin, meaning "outside of the temple"). Perhaps there is an analogy here. The Bible has no smile in it because the entire story of God's redemption of non-smiling humanity (from Genesis thru Revelation) is one big smile. It is all sacred time–God's time. We can put on a happy face because God in Jesus the Christ has set things right between us and God the Father. We are that baby in the crib upon whom God smiles. So when you next walk into Cazenovia's United Methodist Church, smile, you are on God's Time.

September 2014

"Teacher, Teacher..."

It is September. The kids are back in school, much to the relief of their parents. By the end of summer, some youngsters began singing the "I'm bored" song, so to have them out of the house and in the classroom is a welcome change. Moms and Dads get a break now as teachers take over the role of parents. According to their job description, teachers are *"in parentis locus,"* a Latin phrase meaning that the educators of our children act with parental authority and responsibility in the classroom. This implies that teachers are to model exemplary behavior, ethics, and morality.

Frances Nelson, a teacher of English (Communication Skills) at Coshocton High School, Coshocton, Ohio, calculated that she and others in her profession have "7 hours a day for 180 days a year to influence: 1,260 hours a year. Total this time by 12 years, and the time is immense: 15,120 hours for teachers to make a difference in the life of a child."

School boards expect much of those whom they employ to shape the lives of young people. I suspect that educators today feel overburdened by regulatory authorities. I know that some chafe at the "teach to standards" movement that has put so great an emphasis on testing. Still, contemporary educators should give a collective sigh of relief that they are not bound to the "Rules for Teachers" put in place in 1877 by the School Board responsible for the Neales Flat School near Eudunda in southern Australia. Here are the rules:

1. Teachers each day will fill lamps, clean chimneys.

2. Each teacher will bring a bucket of water and a scuttle of coal for the day's session.

3. Make your pens carefully. You whittle nibs to the individual taste of the pupils.

4. Men teachers may take one evening a week for courting purposes, or two evenings a week if they go to church regularly.

5. After 10 hours in school, the teachers may spend the remaining time reading the Bible or other good books.

6. Women teachers who marry or engage in unseemly conduct will be dismissed.

7. Every teacher should lay aside from each pay a goodly sum of his earnings for his benefit during his declining years so he will not become a burden on society.

8. Any teacher who smokes, uses liquor in any form, frequents pool or public halls, or gets shaved in a barbershop will give reason to suspect his worth, intention, integrity and honesty.

9. The teacher who performs his labor faithfully and without fault for five years will be given an increase of two shillings and sixpence per week in his pay providing the Board of Education approves.

Given the severity of these "rules for teachers," I suspect that some who signed on to teach in Neales Flat felt more like hired hands than respected educators.

It may be so today, as the public's expectations of teachers are muddled and contradictory. We want teachers to act professionally (be good role models), but we treat them as employees. We turn our children over to their care, but we do not care enough to collaborate with them so that classroom expectations are reinforced at home. I can remember a time when membership in the PTA was expected of everyone who brought a child to school. Nowadays, many PTA groups have a difficult time mustering parental support. Founded in 1897 in Washington, DC, the PTA began as the National Congress of Mothers under the leadership of Alice McLellan Birney and Phoebe Apperson. In the decades that followed, the PTA championed kindergarten classes, hot lunch programs, mandatory immunization, and called on mothers (and fathers) everywhere to improve the lives of children by becoming partners in their education. Today we hear of the PTA's decline. Many parents seem willing to pass on their responsibilities—adopting the position "let the schools do it." Ironically, this is taking place simultaneously with a decline in the respect given teachers by the public.

September is a good month to rethink our understanding of what it means to be a "teacher" and of our need to respect, honor, and support good teachers everywhere, including in our churches. A Sunday School teacher is no less an important role model for your child than the woman (or man) to whom you entrust your third-grader in the public school. The Hebrew word for teacher--"rabbi" --carries distinction in the Bible. Though Jesus was technically not a "rabbi," that is, a doctor of religious law, his disciples and others often addressed him as such. For example, we read:

"Now there was a man of the Pharisees, named Nicodemus, a ruler of the Jews. This man came to Jesus by night and said to Him, "Rabbi, we know that You are a teacher come from God; for no one can do these signs that You do, unless God is with him." (John 3:1-2 RSV)

October 2014

Christian Croquet, Anyone?

Football season is upon us. Men in helmets and shoulder pads butt heads while other men (and some women) cheer from the sidelines clutching a Golden Molson in one hand and the television remote control in the other. I had a moment of glory once on the ol' gridiron back in Hampton, Iowa, when I was trying out for a second string end position with my high school team—the

mighty Bulldogs. Joe Jennings, our junior varsity quarterback, threw the long bomb. I caught it and gazelle-like danced into the end zone. No defensive player touched me. I was ecstatic. In the second quarter, by some fluke of the gods of sport, I caught a Jennings pass again. This time Mark Geddes, a really big boy whose dad ran the local milk dairy plant and sold ice cream cones for 5 cents a piece, hit me—and hard. I went down feeling as if one of Papa Geddes's milk trucks had run over me. On that day, I learned two lessons—I don't like pain and football involves a lot of pain.

In subsequent years, I looked for a non-contact sport at which I had a chance to excel. I thought it might be tennis, since I usually beat my younger brother on our hometown court—a concrete affair with grass growing profusely out of the cracks. But when Jan and I began dating in college, she routinely beat me at tennis, having had a college class in tennis. Badminton then became my forte, until a stickler for the rules pointed out that it wasn't legal to reach over the net. I tried volleyball too, was good at the sport, and was convinced that I had found my calling. Then I saw a match between the Chinese national women's team and the Syracuse University women. The shortest Chinese player could have spiked me into the ground.

Now at the age of 72, I have, at last, found my sport. I shall call it Christian Croquet, to borrow a phrase coined by Rick Bohlke. Rick was among the group of husbands who once accompanied members of my wife's monthly Bunco club who came to our house. While the women played Bunco indoors, we men set up a Croquet game in the back yard. Though the verbal exchanges echoed loudly in the gathering darkness and several of my good friends got a bit heated when Ralph Richmond played according to the Rules of Ralph rather than anything Milton Bradley might have written in his 1871 publication Croquet—Its Principles and Rules, no one was injured. Except to the loser's ego, Croquet is a pain free sport. The clumsy may, of course, bruise a foot with an inept stroke. But this is not the essence of the game. By way of contrast, knocking your opponent on his behind is part of football.

This raises a theological issue for our best minds. Are there some sports that are more Christian than others? This is not an entirely facetious question, especially in the American culture where sports heroes are treated like gods and millions worship at the Shrine of Monday Night Football. I suspect that in some parts of the country (places like Kilgore, Texas) football **is** religion. Coaches and players huddle together in prayer before the big game. Local preachers give their (and presumably, God's blessing) to the home team. Then the young men are sent out onto the playing field to maul and maim. Football enthusiasts will argue that mauling and maiming are not the main goals of the game. They are right, of course, but I've yet to see a hard fought football game with the participants acting as if they were at a country hoe down doing the square dance. What must go through a 300 lb. born-again Christian offensive tackle's mind as he slams into the defensive tackle opposite him— "Jesus loves you, and so do I. Bam! You've got a broken nose!"?

Lest you think my dour musings about football stem from deep emotional trauma occasioned by that hit from Mark Geddes decades ago, I hasten to add that I have cheered for the Syracuse University Orange and for the Buffalo Bills too. Still, I am left to wonder about the facile connection in our culture between religion and sport. Too many Americans make sport their substitute church, be it football, baseball, or golf—they vicariously find self-affirmation in having their team trounce the opponent. In spite of all of the pious rhetoric about being a good loser, most boys in the Pop Warner leagues want to grow up and be winners. Some sports junkies become dependent personalities, and when their team loses they feel like losers in life. Occasionally, the passion for winning borders on the criminal. Those European soccer fans who routinely riot and pummel the supporters of the other side are a major menace to the good name of soccer.

Contrary to pre-Olympics speculation, the 2004 Games in Athens, Greece, were a success. No terrorist attacks. No major scandals. I did find the opening and closing ceremonies to be a bit too theatrical, with those Greek gods flying about over the heads of the participants. The ancient Greeks, as St. Paul discovered when he preached in Athens, believed in multiple divinities. Their Olympian pantheon consisted of twelve gods and goddesses, such as Hera and Hermes, who sported among themselves. Classical Greek myths portray the gods as superhuman beings intent upon having a good time. Game playing is heavenly sport.

By way of contrast, the Hebrew Bible gives scant attention to sport. If the ancient Jews played games, their writers and prophets tell us little about them. The New Testament is remarkably silent about gaming. Jesus is never depicted participating in an athletic sport. His mission was of a higher order. As our substitute, he fought the good fight, defeating both the devil and death. This cosmic battle resulted in Christ as the Victor, champion of all lost souls, even those of us who will never wear an Olympic gold medal, much less, get our name as winners on the local sports page. Christ's crown of thorns is our crown of gold. Wear it proudly.

November 2014

Ragamuffin

By a less commonly used dictionary definition, I grew up an orphan. The word itself now seems antiquated, bringing to mind scenes from old movies based on Charles Dickens' description of life in the London slums during the grim and sooty industrial 19th-century. Ragamuffins in tattered clothing, their stomachs aching from hunger, loll about the streets, while the rich and privileged ride by in comfortable splendor. My own picture of what it would be like to be on my own at age eight was of the unfortunates who were sent to the Orphan's Home down at Davenport, Iowa. Established soon after the Civil War, this institution cared primarily for the children of soldiers who died at places like Bull Run and Chickamauga Creek. In later decades, Iowa kids who lost their parents (or even one parent, as I had) were sometimes declared "wards of the State" and placed in the Davenport orphanage. I sometimes had bad dreams about being among the neglected at Davenport.

In one scenario, it is Thanksgiving. We orphans sit around long wooden tables waiting for our dinner. Davenport's Orphan's Home is no workhouse where children slave for food by doing menial labor, as was the custom in the older English system. We have our social workers, our teachers, and our nurses. Moreover, today, this wonderful Thanksgiving Day, we have the cooks. Mouth-watering odors waft from the huge kitchen off the common room.

We grasp our knives and forks in eager anticipation. Mrs. Harmon and Mrs. Avery, large ladies in white aprons, bring in the traditional main course. Turkey. But it is only <u>one</u> turkey! And an undernourished one at that! One hundred boys and one puny bird! I wake up in a panic.

Today orphanages of the kind at Davenport are rare. We have come to understand something of the damage done by institutional regimentation. Where children without parents cannot be adopted or placed in foster homes, government agencies assist with the maintenance of the so-called cottage system. These group homes attempt to duplicate the model of family as closely as possible. Religious groups and other charitable organizations operate a number of them. My mother gave generously for years to the work of Father Edward Flanagan at Boys Town, Nebraska. Established by the young priest in 1917 when he took in homeless boys, Boys Town was made famous by the movie in 1938 in which Spencer Tracy played Father Flanagan and Mickey Rooney came under his care. I saw the movie and thought, "If I must go someplace, send me to Boys Town." I knew they had a farm there. Raised turkeys too.

This Thanksgiving the local news will bring us familiar images from Syracuse's Rescue Mission of the traditional turkey dinner. A few years ago, Clarence Jordan retired after forty years at the helm of the Rescue Mission. I was one of his secret admirers for a long time and still have a hard time thinking of the Rescue Mission without him in the top post. His blend of Christian compassion and social action strikes me as the right recipe for our day when it is easy to become complacent under the mistaken assumption that the government watches out for the "least and the lost." Clarence knew his Bible well and would be the first to call our attention to the Old Testament custom of sharing one's bounty with those who have less. In the Book of Deuteronomy (24:19), this is the law which Moses set before the children of Israel: "When you reap your harvest in your field you shall not go back to get it; it shall be for the sojourner, the fatherless, and the widow, that the Lord your God may bless you in all the work of your hands."

In ancient times, villagers went into the wheat fields to gather grain left behind by the reapers. Both church and state recognized the gleaning rights of the peasants. In this age when overproduction and inequities in the world market result in huge stockpiles of wheat, so that a bushel of hard red wheat brings a farmer in Kansas less than the cost of a loaf of bread, we can do more than offer widows and orphans the leftovers. There are many agencies, such as C.R.O.P. and OxFarm, which attempt to bring a portion of America's cornucopia to the hungry of the world. Closer to home, we have channels through which to enlarge the Thanksgiving table, including Syracuse's Rescue Mission.

It will come as something of a surprise to my brother Gilbert and sister Laureen to read that I once thought of myself as but a wishbone away from being an orphan or ragamuffin. Father did indeed leave mother a widow when I was in the second grade, and by Webster's lesser known definition of the word, we little Sernetts were orphans. Except for my nighttime musings about the home at Davenport, I grew up without the fear of loneliness those who are truly without family must face every day, and, perhaps more painfully, on special occasions such as Thanksgiving when we are sweetly smothered by the Norman Rockwell sentiment of the happy extended family gathered around the groaning harvest table.

Yet in all of us there is a deep rooted terror of being abandoned, symptom of the sinful state, I suppose. Therefore, it is with great thanksgiving that we remember at this time of the year our adoption into the family of God, to whom every one of us is a favored child.

December 2014

To Truss a Goose

I recall the Christmas when an Episcopalian clergy woman told the nativity story to a Lutheran congregation. That was back in 1996 when Ecumenical conversations were going on between Lutherans and Episcopalians. Jan and I were then 100 per cent Lutheran as opposed to being 50 per cent Lutheran and 50 per cent Methodist as we are today. I welcomed the news of a Lutheran/Espicopalian engagement. Any advance on the frontier of Christian union ought to be

celebrated, but this yoking of traditions has its special virtues--especially as we entered into the holiday season.

I grew up with the notion that the English have more food and fun at Christmas than Americans and most all of the best stories. Think of the British tradition of "wassailing" --wherein rosy-cheeked celebrants toast "good health" with a beverage made of eggs, mulled ale, roasted apples, curdled cream, nuts and spices. Credit Merry Old England with the roasted boar's head, the hanging of holly, and plum pudding. The custom of exchanging Christmas cards began with the one-penny postal service in 1840. Sir Henry Cole offered the first commercially produced cards in 1846. Savor the prospect of Yorkshire Pudding and Mincemeat Pie--the British have it all--even the Christmas tree. Prince Albert, himself a German, popularized this custom (attributed to Luther) when in 1841 he set up a tree in Windsor Castle in to the delight of Queen Victoria and the royal family. I was encouraged to campaign for an old-fashioned Charles Dickens Christmas in our household. You know--the kind of Christmas dinner that Tiny Tim and the rest of the Bob

Cratchit family sat down to in "A Christmas Carol" after Old Scrooge repented of his miserly ways. This means Christmas goose--not chicken, turkey or any fowl of the offbeat variety (such as partridge) but a big, fat goose.

Fat may have been the problem, for the majority of the Sernetts judged goose to be too greasy, therefore unhealthy, yea even "yucky." So I secretly boned up on a recipe for roast goose with sage and onion stuffing--as in the classic by Dickens. Dickens wrote: "There never was such a goose. Bob said he didn't believe there ever was such a goose cooked. Its tenderness and flavor, size and cheapness, were themes of universal admiration. Eked out by applesauce and mashed potatoes, it was a sufficient dinner for the whole family." My goal of an English Christmas dinner as in the days of yore ran afoul on technical grounds. I didn't know how to truss a Goose. I'm told that geese have shorter legs than chickens and turkeys, making the business of tying everything together more difficult. Amateurs who savor the taste of roast goose are well advised to do their homework. A little practice makes perfect. No one wants goose giblets in their Figgie pudding. There's an old adage that the food we eat tells much about us, so I won't pursue this Christmas goose much further.

William Bolitho once wrote from London, "Christmas in England is fundamental. Russia, Spain, keep Easter. France has New Years. In mysterious, sentimental Germany, they have a Christmas of their own, but I suspect birthdays and marriage anniversaries are bigger feasts. Here we have only Christmas." I take Bolitho to mean that the English invest so much in the holiday season that they risk overindulging. Victorian England in the days of Dickens was intoxicated with Christmas. Hearty good feeling and high living overwhelmed the voices of the angels heralding the incarnation in the birth of a carpenter's son there in Bethlehem. Too much plum pudding and Christmas goose can lead to spiritual dyspepsia.

So where does this lead us? Would a peanut butter and jelly sandwich for Christmas dinner be spiritually more satisfying--on the principle that less is more? I'm not so sure. An advocate of moderation in all things, I look for the golden mean. I discount the notion of Christmas all the year round and its opposite, the proposition that Christmas festivities are dangerous to the health of body and soul. If goose is too rich for you and peanut butter and jelly toast too lean, then go for the Risotto Con Frutti Di Mare--that's Italian for rice with shellfish. If Lutherans and Anglicans can sit together at the Christmas table, then Roman Catholics are soon to come. One wonders what John Wesley's wife, Mary or Molly as she was known, served at Christmas. All we know is that she left John in 1758 after seven years of marriage.

The true meaning of Christmas is in the universal divine love feast. "And the angel said unto them, Fear not: for, behold, I bring you good tidings of great joy, which shall be to all people." St. Luke 2: 10

So come to the table this Christmas and rejoice in the plentitude of God's gift of love in the Infant born "away in a manger."

January 2015

Finding Your Way in 2015

When our son Matthew first began to drive, he navigated willy-nilly by setting off in the general direction of his quarry on the assumption that by driving long enough he was sure to hit upon something. Some people have a hard time asking for directions. I read of an elderly couple in New Jersey who wanted to drive to the dentist. The husband was one these males who on principle (sheer stubbornness) refuses to ask for guidance from a stranger. So on he drove, despite his wife's pleadings, hour after hour until the couple crossed the state line several hundred miles from their original destination.

When I read the story in the press, I thought back to a trip my mother and I took back in the 1950s with Uncle Charlie and Aunt Elsie from northern Iowa up to Minneapolis for the Minnesota State Fair. Aunt Elsie drove, as the green Chrysler was her car, paid for with the egg money. To ride with Aunt Elsie was always an adventure. These were the days when Iowa had no posted speed limit. The Chrysler could do eighty on the gravel roads and kick up a beautiful chicken tail of dust and stone. Once we got into Minneapolis, however, Aunt Elsie slowed down. We were in foreign territory without a clue as to the location of the fairgrounds. My aunt refused to ask for directions, so we spent a good share of the day cruising around looking for the farm show.

Christians worldwide celebrate January 6th as the Epiphany. The Eastern Orthodox Church observes the day as the anniversary of the baptism of Jesus, while here in the Western church we think of Epiphany as commemorating the revelation  to the Gentiles of Jesus Christ as the Savior as told in the story of the coming of the Magi, or Three Wise Men. (Matthew 2:1-12) These noble pilgrims are said to have been of the priestly caste in ancient Persia (contemporary Iran) and believers in Zoroastrianism. Tradition has it that their names were Casper, Melchior and Balthazar. We sing of them in "We Three Kings of Orient are . . .", and many a Sunday School child has brought "gold, frankincense and myrrh" to Bethlehem's manger as modern-day magi.

The three original wise men had no road maps to follow. The nearest AAA office with those handy Triptiks was centuries away. GPS systems were far into the future. Caspar, Melchior and Balthazar, or whatever their names were, had to cross miles and miles of desert with not an oasis is sight. They did have a star. When I was small, I would look up into the Iowa sky each Christmas Eve in the hope of seeing that same star. Twinkle, Twinkle, Little Star. But which star? I am to this day astronomically challenged. I can show you the Big Dipper but cannot tell you where to look for Orion or Ursa Major. Had I been one of the wise men and told to follow a star, I would have said, "Which star?"

Starting out on a new year is like setting off on a great journey without a map. We fill in the trip diary as we go. All we know in advance is that there will be many a crossroad where decisions, maybe even life and death ones, must be made. Because life is an adventure, it is risky business. Ancient travelers like the Magi knew that every sojourn entailed danger. Bands of highwaymen roamed about eager to strip their small caravan of the precious gifts they were bringing to the Christ Child. When I drive down Ridge Road into Cazenovia, I am generally not thinking about the possibility that robbers will rush the car and demand my money. But I have had enough "near miss" encounters with other drivers and their vehicles over the years to know that accidents are waiting to happen.

"The Story of the Other Wise Man" by Henry Van Dyke teaches us how to live life with a surer sense of direction. Van Dyke tells of a forth wise man, an astronomer and physician by the name of Artaban. Artaban wishes to bring a sapphire, a ruby and a pearl to the Christ Child but fails to join up with the other Magi because along the way he is delayed. The sapphire is given to help other wayfarers cross the desert. The ruby goes to save the life of a small child, and the gift of the pearl keeps a young woman from being sold into slavery. Artaban searches for the Christ for almost thirty-three years. A Jewish Rabbi counsels him that the Kingdom of God will not be found among the rich and powerful but is the royalty of perfect and unconquerable love. At the end of the story, Artaban is in Jerusalem at the time of the Passover. A crucifixion is taking place. The sky darkens. The earth shakes. A heavy tile strikes and bloodies Artaban, and he seems to be whispering, "not so, My Lord, for when did I see you hungry, or thirsty and gave thee to drink? When did I see a stranger and take thee in? For 33 years I have looked for you and never saw your face." Then Artaban hears a voice saying, "as often as you did it to one of these, my brethren, you did it to me."

I don't have a road map to offer you for 2015. But I can suggest that if we adopt the spirit of loving demonstrated by Artaban we will in the end find our way. We can make the journey less burdensome by being willing to ask for advice. Some folks have natural talents like an innate sense of direction. Should you need help getting from point A to point B, then remember what the Bible says, "And a little child will lead them . . ."

And there in front of them was the star they had seen rising.
It went forward and halted over the place where the child was. . .

They saw the child with his mother Mary, and falling to their knees
they did him homage.
Matthew 2:9-12

"He Belongs to The Angels, Now"

When Abraham Lincoln's great heart stopped at approximately twenty-two minutes past seven o'clock on April 15, 1865, there were no television cameras or tape recorders there to document his passing. Lincoln's pastor, the Reverend Dr. Gurley, stepped forward to lead in prayer. A corporal by the name of James Tanner attempted to capture the benediction on paper, but the point of his pencil caught in his coat and broke. Henry Stanton, Secretary of State, sobbed out the words, "He belongs to the angels now." Though a fitting epitaph for the martyred President, Stanton may not have said this at all. Others recalled that he remarked: "He belongs to the ages." One historian describes this version of Stanton's comment as "loftier."

Since early childhood, I have been drawn to the life and lore of our 16th President whose birthday we observe on the 16th of this month. George Washington ranks no higher in my roster of great Americans. This admiration for Lincoln is difficult to account for, though teaching in Springfield, Illinois, for three years with ready access to his home and grave enriched a passion in me that took root in elementary school when I read a book about Lincoln's funeral train as it carried his earthly remains on the long trip home to Springfield.

Lincoln was not religious in the conventional 19th-century sense. He attended Presbyterian services in Springfield and in Washington, D. C., but never joined any denomination. He reasoned: "When any church shall inscribe over its altar, as its sole qualification for membership, the Savior's condensed statement of the substance of both Law and Gospel, 'Thou shalt love the Lord thy God with all thy heart, and with all thy soul, and with all thy mind, and thy neighbor, as thyself,' that church will I join with all my heart and all my soul."

Reluctant to embrace any of the competing creeds of the day, Lincoln was sometimes a target for ridicule in the camp of the traditionalists. His skepticism was sorely tested by the death of his son Willie. The President fell into a deep depression and twice had Willie's tomb opened so he could look upon him again. Lincoln's religious views deepened as the burden of being President increased. "In the present civil war," he wrote in 1862, "it is quite possible that God's purpose is something different from the purpose of either party--and yet the human instrumentalities, working just as they do, are of the best adaptation to effect His purpose." Whether conscious of it or not, the president whom John Wilkes Booth would cut down at Ford's theater but a few days after Lee surrendered to Grant at Appomattox Courthouse, was fashioning a doctrine of providence.

I have not heard a sermon on providence with a big "P" in a long time. With all of the political turmoil these days, perhaps preachers are gun shy of attempting to convey what God's intentions are. We have no modern-day equivalent of the court chaplain, much less wizards armed with power to search out the deeper meaning of current events. The ancient Greeks tried to chart the future by divining the entrails of birds. Here Providence and Fate conjoined, and mortals thought of their destinies as governed by the stars.

While the New Testament has no word to represent the popular notion of providence, there is something in the Gospel of Matthew that is instructive and close to Lincoln's understanding of Providence. Jesus says: "Are not two sparrows sold for a penny? And not one of them will fall to the ground without your Father's will. But even the hairs of your head are numbered. Fear not, therefore; you are of more value than many sparrows." In the midst of a dreadful national conflict, when the daily newspapers portrayed death upon death, Lincoln fell back upon an understanding of history rooted in Biblical testimony. God created the world, governs it, and cares for its welfare.

With all of this in mind, I am not too concerned about which version of Stanton's remarks historians claim to be accurate. Both would be in character with Lincoln the Man and Lincoln the President. Lincoln's greatness derives in part from his understanding of the responsibilities of being president at so critical a time in the history of the nation. He believed that God's will for good was expressed through the instrumentality of humans. In this sense, history and the angels came together for the good of all. One cannot escape responsibility (and culpability) for one's actions.

In some ways, I wish I were back in my High School Civics class in 1959. Our teacher tried to instill respect for the American system in our thick heads and uncaring souls while battling cancer on the personal front. He would have understood Lincoln's greatness and cherished Lincoln's ability to see the Hand of God in even the most trying of circumstances.

March 2015

Keep Your Fork!

There was a woman who had been diagnosed with a terminal illness and had been given three months to live. Therefore, as she was getting her things "in order," she contacted her pastor and had him come to her house to discuss certain aspects of her final wishes. She told him which songs she wanted sung at the service, what scriptures she would like read, and what outfit she wanted to be buried in. The woman also requested to be buried with her favorite Bible. Everything was in order and the pastor was preparing to leave when the woman suddenly remembered something very important to her.

"There's one more thing," she said excitedly.

"What's that?" came the pastor's reply.

"This is very important," the woman continued, "I want to be buried with a fork in my right hand."

The pastor stood looking at the woman, not knowing quite what to say . . .

"That surprises you, doesn't it?" the woman asked.

"Well, to be honest, I'm puzzled by the request," said the pastor.

The woman explained. "In all my years of attending church socials and potluck dinners, I always remember that when the dishes of the main course were being cleared, someone would inevitably lean over and say, 'keep your fork.' It was my favorite part because I knew that something better was coming, like velvety chocolate cake or deep-dish apple pie. Something wonderful, and with substance!

So, I just want people to see me there in that casket with a fork in my hand and I want them to wonder 'What's with the fork?' Then I want you to tell them: "Keep Your Fork. The best is yet to come."

The pastor's eyes welled up with tears of joy as he hugged the woman when saying goodbye. He knew this would be one of the last times he would see her before her death. Nevertheless, he also knew that the woman had a better grasp of heaven than he did. She KNEW that something better was coming. At the funeral, people walked by the woman's casket and saw the pretty dress she was wearing and her favorite Bible and the fork placed in her right hand. Repeatedly the pastor heard the question "What's with the fork?" And over and over he smiled.

During his message, the pastor told the people of the conversation he had with the woman shortly before she died. He also told them about the fork and about what it symbolized to her. The pastor told the people how he could not stop thinking about the fork and told them that they probably would not be able to stop thinking about it either. He was right. Therefore, the next time you reach down for your fork, let it remind you, oh so gently, that the best is yet to come!

This story about the woman with the fork is not mine, though I wish it were. For it captures our Lenten mood here in March. Since Ash Wednesday in February, we have been in penitential preparation for Easter. In apostolic times the Lenten season was when candidates for baptism exercised discipline of body and mind in anticipation of Easter morning when they joined the fellowship of believers. In some Christian communities today, fasting is observed during the forty days between Ash Wednesday and Easter (Sundays excepted). Except for those times when I have had to fast because of an impending blood test, I haven't gone without food for very long. Thus I can't offer any insight on the spiritual value of fasting, though some of you who grew up in the Roman Catholic church and remember "meatless Fridays" may want to witness to the soul-enriching benefits of doing without.

My recollections are more in keeping with those of the woman with the fork. Years ago we would troop down to the basement of Trinity Lutheran Church back there in Hampton, Iowa, whenever there was a church dinner. Our Lutheran ladies, many of them farm women who loved to cook, understood the power of deferred gratification. I would sit through a lot of boring meetings as a kid in anticipation of what would come once the sliding window went up. And yes, after the fried chicken, baked beans, mashed potatoes, and orange Jell-O with little floating marshmallows, out came the best–pie and ice cream. We kept our forks of course.

Keep your forks this month. The best is yet to come– "something wonderful and with substance."

Easter arrives on Sunday, April 5!

April 2015

Your Easter Compass

I knew a young man from Iowa who got his inner compass stuck. Normally he went through life with a mental quirk, whereby something in the back of his mind was, as Ronald Jager, philosopher-historian and Midwest product himself puts it, "always busy noting directions, making corrections, generating constant low-level interest and information about north-south-east-west." Jager contends that those of us who grew up within the graveled grid of rural Middle America have a "livelier inner compass" than, for example, New Englanders, whose roads twist and turn in endless confusion. Folks with an inner compass live in houses square with the world; they have a ready answer to the question, "Which way seems North?" Folks who are not so gifted or burdened can go for days without worrying about or even being conscious of directions. When lost, they simply head for the nearest gas station and are steered to their destination. In contrast, the inner compass crowd always seems to know north from south and east from west, that is, until something sets their mental apparatus askew.

My inner compass went haywire when I was twelve. It was a traumatic experience for a lad who was taught to plant peas in straight rows aligned with the rising and setting of the sun and who believed that he could always find home (or his starting point) by making three right turns. That summer I was helping Uncle Charlie put up hay when we took a break on a rainy day and visited Mystery Cave in Southern Minnesota. The cavern descent took us deep into the dark earth; there, hundreds of feet beneath checkerboard fields of corn and beans, we contorted through a snarl of tunnels. I emerged disorientated; my inner compass had swung off true north. For days, I went about in a daze, confused by a sun that rose in the south and set in the north. I dreaded being by myself for fear I might set off to feed the hogs in the north pasture and end up at the South Pole.

When our inner compass is set on Christ, permanently so, then all our words and deeds reflect His Glory. Hear these words from the hymn "Shine Jesus Shine": "As we gaze on your kingly brightness, so our faces display your likeness, ever changing from glory to glory, mirrored here, may our lives tell your story." It is easy to be an Easter Christian, showing up for the grand finale of the Church Year when winter's days, dark and dour, have given way to the light airiness of early spring. It is more difficult to follow the Stations of the Cross leading to Good Friday and the closing of the book of life at a traditional Tenebrae service.

During the hours between the end of our Good Friday service and Easter morning, I am reminded of how I felt down in that dark cave at the age of twelve. It seems to be a "time out of time"—an eerie and unsettling stretch when I think the earth might wobble in its customary orbit and things go "wackety-wack." Then I distrust intuition and so shun new projects, for fear that the fundamental laws of geometry, not to mention domestic science, have been suspended. Neither the carpenter's square nor the cook's measuring cup can be trusted. When life's master template is being tested, why mess with constructing a new crib for the baby or baking twelve-layer lasagna. I suppose this is how dwellers on the slopes of Vesuvius felt when they heard that a mountain of hot lava was flowing their way.

Praise God! there is reason to hope. Easter morning crowns our waiting. The sun rises in the East! And once again our inner moral compass rights itself. Mine did after that death-like cave experience at the age of twelve when I returned home to Hampton, got into my own house, my own bedroom, my own bed. I went to sleep confused and clueless but arose the next morning in familiar surroundings, with the sun ascending in the east, blessing mother's rhubarb and the wash hung on the line. Now everything appeared "true"—north was north, etc. So it is with our Easter experience. No matter how far you have strayed, no matter what subterranean detours you have taken, you can come home again. Look to Easter this April 5th. There shall your Salvation be.

Awake, all souls that sleep.
Across the year but once or twice
Can men hear angels calling.
Heed that first trumpet, nor await the last.
The resurrection moment soon is past.
Life calls again, to all that would be living,
(John Slater)

Mud in May, and Other Simple Gospel Pleasures

Karen Armstrong, an academic theologian with sterling credentials, once joined a Roman Catholic order of sisters in search of spiritual enlightenment. She left and later reported that she had done so because she had been unable to "find God." People who say that they are trying to "find God" may be surprised one day to discover that God has found them. Think of Paul on the road to Damascus, John Wesley at Aldersgate, or Luther caught in that thunderstorm. In these examples, faith and commitment came unexpectedly as a breath of fresh air blowing upon dying embers. After their respective encounters with God, Martin Luther, John Wesley, and especially St. Paul became aflame for the Lord. Their lives were irrevocably altered.

I think of the month of May as a time of refreshing and renewal. Winter has receded. It is time for spring-cleaning. Sweep out the garage, put up the clotheslines, and wash the car. There is lightness in the air—a sense of new possibilities. The old emerge from winter hibernation, feeling rejuvenated and, for a brief time, at least, letting the child in them come to the surface. Who does not recall with pleasure how it felt to be young and free at the start of summer? Try now to put yourself back in time to the age of five, in the month of May, on a day just after a refreshing spring rain. You are let outdoors and allowed to run barefoot in the backyard. If your imagination is vivid enough, perhaps you can become the little child in Polly Chase Boyden's poem.

Mud is very nice to feel
All squishy-squash between the toes!
I'd rather wade in wiggly mud
Than smell a yellow rose
Nobody else but the rosebush knows
How nice mud feels
Between the toes.

I occasionally ask my wife if she would like to reverse time and become once again that little girl growing up on a farm in northern Illinois. Her response has always been no—not because she had an unhappy childhood or any particularly traumatic experience during her early years, but because she knows that we cannot relive our lives. By way of contrast, I often muse on the possibility of becoming that Iowa lad I once was. Of course, I qualify this nostalgic bit of whimsy with the proviso that I would want to go back in time "knowing what I know now." Jan is quick to point out how implausible and unworkable such a desire is. If I relived that childhood in light of my adult self, it would not be the childhood I had known and now remember with such fondness. It is a paradox without any resolution.

Our faith lives can seem to contain a similar paradox. When we are young, believing comes easily. Our Sunday school teacher tells us that before we go to sleep each night we should say:

Matthew, Mark, Luke, and John
Bless the bed that I lie on.
Before I lay me down to sleep
I give my soul to Christ to keep.
Four corners to my bed,
Four angels there aspread,
Two to foot, and two to head,
And four to carry me when I'm dead.
I go by sea, I go by land,
The Lord made me with His right hand.
If any danger come to me,
Sweet Jesus Christ deliver me.
He's the branch and I'm the flower,
Pray God send me a happy hour,
And if I die before I wake,
I pray that Christ my soul to take.

Then we grow up, become adults, and our childlike faith slips away or ossifies like the bones of the dead.

It is not too late to throw open the windows of your heart and experience once more the refreshing spirit of the Lord. God will find you in whatever adult wilderness you have become lost.

So kick off your shoes, feel the mud between your toes.

Pray the prayers of the child within you.

June 2015

On the Power of Prayer

In the best-selling Mitford series by author Jan Karon, Father Tim, an Episcopal priest serving a small parish in a village located in North Carolina's Blue Mountains, is attacked by a huge dog. He eventually discovers that the very large and overly friendly canine, mostly Bouvier, but with a mix of wild Irish wolfhound and sheep dog, can only be controlled by quoting scripture at him. When Barnabas (the dog) attempts to place his paws on the diminutive priest's shoulders and fog up his glasses with dog slobber, Father Tim, drawing from a deep reservoir of Scripture verses, quotes the Apostle Peter, "Repent and be baptized, every one of you!" Barnabas immediately quiets down. At one point in <u>At Home in Mitford</u> (the first novel in the series), Father Tim merely has to shout the location of a Biblical passage, something like "1 Timothy 2: 14", and the dog is tamed.

Karon's wonderfully written account of the comings and goings of the residents of the imaginary community of Mitford centers on the bachelor rector with the dog the size of a sofa. Father Tim's use of Scripture to domesticate the wild beast made me think about the power of prayer.

While my wife was hospitalized some years back, she received many expressions of support. Well-wishers asserted, "We'll say a little prayer for you," or words to that effect. I thought to myself, "What not a big prayer? We need a full dose here! This isn't like making a cup a weak coffee. I recalled that when my brother's wife had surgery she had the support of something called the Bible Baptist Bus Drivers Prayer Circle. One of these ladies came each school day, even in the winter when the sun was not yet up, to transport my niece to her special education classes. Somehow the word got out that Erica's mother was having surgery and before long an entire fleet of Bible Baptist Bus Drivers in Southern Michigan was on the case. It worked.

I do not wish to slight the good folks who visited Jan while she was hospitalized. The Rev. Jim Shaud, our Lutheran pastor at the time, came by, as did two (Why two?) Methodist clergy. Jan was grateful for their prayerful support, as was I. Still, I could not get those Bible Baptist Bus Drivers out of my mind. I am not sure why I secretly thought of calling my brother and finding out if maybe, just maybe, those bus driver ladies had room for another name on their prayer list. I do not believe that God listens more readily to the prayers of Baptists than to the supplications of Lutherans or Methodists. Perhaps it was the bus driver business.

My father-in-law, in an attempt to supplement his farm income, drove a bus for the public school in Union, Illinois, for a number of years. It was a trying experience for Erv, and he voluntarily retired from an occupation more hazardous than working around a grain elevator at full throttle. Put a bunch of kids into one of those yellow transports and hunker down. Neither the patience of Job or the devotion of Mother Teresa suffices. Driving a school bus must be something like trying to fend off a huge, overly aggressive dog. In one of the Mitford stories, Father Tim, while attempting to open his office door, is blind sided by Barnabas. Karon writes of the priest, "If he were a cussing man, . . . this would offer a premier opportunity to indulge himself."

Cussing is not the same as praying, however. I am no connoisseur of cussing, having been taught by a pious mother that anyone who must resort to swearing in order to express themselves betrays a lack of knowledge of the richness of the English language. Actually, my mother told me that swearing was dumb and stupid, and, besides, I was not to take the name of the Lord in vain. Despite this lack of practical experience, I have noticed that cussing can be measured by magnitude. Some forms now seem acceptable even in polite company (Oh My God!), while stronger stuff (*!&!#) must be bleeped out on the evening television news. There are, in short, degrees of cussing. Some cursers, such as the men who drove those big earth moving machines when I worked on the Franklin County road survey team as a lad, elevated the art of bad language to so potent a level that my ears burned.

Now prayer is a different medium. Despite the beliefs of many, a prayer on your behalf by the Pope is no more efficacious than that of the Postman. God does not judge the worthiness of an appeal on the behalf of one who suffers according to the rank or status of the supplicant. I believe that God is radically egalitarian when sorting through the millions of petitions which each day are sent heavenward by humans of all sorts and conditions. Some prayers sound silly (like those voiced by football teams as they are about to beat their opponents to a pulp), while others, say of the child with leukemia asking for a Teddy Bear at Christmas, are compelling, but who are we to judge? I envy those who when asked on the spur of the moment to say a word of prayer at a public gathering, can manage literate verse worthy of Shakespeare himself. My spontaneous prayers usually sound like the first draft of badly written paragraph.

The secret of effective prayer is not in the pray-er at all. In At Home in Mitford, Father Tim is paid a visit by a character called Uncle Billy, whose wife Miss Rose suffers from schizophrenia. Uncle Billy tells Father Tim that the couple has sought help for Miss Rose from the Baptists, the Methodists, and the Presbyterians. Nothing has worked. Though these mountain folk have grown up with shouting preachers and loud revivals, they've become desperate enough to try the Episcopalians. Uncle Billy worries about the "all th' kneeling' and gettin' up and down an all" at Lord's Chapel, but Father Tim says, "You know you don't have to kneel. You can stand or you can sit, just as well. Jesus prayed in both those ways." As to helping Miss Rose, Father Tim tells Uncle Billy, "Our church can't heal Miss Rose any more than the Methodists or the Baptists can. Only God can heal. But we'll do all we can, you have my word."

So let it be with us.

July 2015

"The Magnificent Sanctuary Band"

July is a grand month for family reunions. The picnic groves and parks of America become sacred ground for the ceremonial gathering of individuals who share a common genetic pool. Some years back, a distant cousin of my wife sounded the call for the Rosenwinkel Family Reunion on July 17, complete with pig roast, at St. Paul Lutheran Church in Addison, Illinois. "Don't miss it!" his postcard shouted. "Never before in the history of the planet has there ever been as large a convergence of Rosenwinkels in one place at one time." The announcement promised instant kinship at the Rosenwinkel Family Reunion--a lot of blue eyes, same noses, same earlobes, and a collection of wild cowlicks, all Rosenwinkel trademarks.

Though a Rosenwinkel only by marriage, I wanted very much to attend this cosmic event, not so much for the taste of roast pig but for the feeling of family, and tribe, and roots. Too many of our families are scattered across the country and the world. Who has not, in visiting a strange city, checked the phone book to find out if relatives (however remote) might live there? I once discovered several listings under "Sernett" (an uncommon surname) in the Minneapolis-St. Paul white pages, thought of ringing the numbers, then desisted on the premise that a call from a perfect stranger might be unwelcome. The desire for belonging, for a shared identity, is very deep in the human soul.

The yearning for community sometimes is expressed in (to my mind) peculiar ways. Annually during the summer, the owners of AIRSTREAM motor homes rally like schools of silver-grey Beluga whales in search of a feeding ground. I am told that the AIRSTREAM family is a close one, with strong loyalty to the AIRSTREAM way of life. Franklin car enthusiasts come to Cazenovia each summer to swap stories and share in the sense of "family" created by titles to vintage air-cooled automobiles once made in Syracuse. It is the price of admission. These days a Franklin in mint condition can cost as much as we sold my mother's house for. A lot of good people are kept out of the Franklin family circle, including yours truly, by the financial barrier.

In protest, I have decided to organize a new, more democratic and cheaper "family" for all who yearn deeply to be members of some club. I hereby announce the "Red Plaid $9.95 Shirt Reunion" for my birthday at the Sernett's on Ridge Road in Cazenovia. Your ticket can be any red plaid shirt (preferably one judged "dorky" by the children) not costing more than $9.95. I bought mine at BJ's Wholesale Club on a whim. We "Red Shirters" have just as much right to annual family reunions as the owners of AIRSTREAM campers or Franklin cars. Once gathered in tribal council, we can make up whatever rules we want. We can elect officers, collect dues, and issue a newsletter.

If the truth were told, I would confess to some nervousness about our "Red Shirt Reunion." What if a gatecrasher showed up--someone in a Green Plaid Long Sleeve Shirt? Would we welcome him around our campfire? The family reunions of today (be they based on the possession of common genetic traits or material objects) are not that far removed from the gathering of tribes in ancient times. Then you did distinguish between friend and foe based on what the stranger was wearing. During battle, Scottish warriors were recognized in the fog of the highland moors by the distinctive plaids of their kilts and tartans.

We live in a world where the pull of tribe is still strong. Witness the youth gangs of our big cities, the ethnic bloodshed that went on in Rwanda and Bosnia, and the political gridlock in Washington caused by loyalty to party rather than principle. Christianity has not been immune to the tribal virus. Denominationalism is the bad fruit of centuries of conflict in the Christian church.

Nevertheless, the local Christian congregation, your "community of saints," stands ready more so than any other human institution to welcome you unconditionally. That is the essence of the Gospel--unconditional acceptance. The reunion of blood relatives--a great gathering of the clan this summer--may be impossible for many of you. For some of us, the phrase "family reunion" rings hollow because of events beyond our control.

Then remember that Fellowship of Christ reunion is each Sunday during the summer. In the words of the old Roy Clark gospel hymn, come join us in "The Magnificent Sanctuary Band."

August 2015

Call Forwarding

If God knows each of us by name, as Isaiah 43:1 implies ("I have called you by name; you are mine."), I wonder what name each of us is called by. None of the apostles or disciples had last names. Peter and Paul; that is all. So how will the good Lord find us if there is need for an urgent message, given the plethora of folks worldwide with common first names?

Names are interesting social placeholders. When you take your car in for repair, the mechanic who works on it wears a shirt or uniform with his first name stitched on it. This seems to be a hallmark of people who work for others, especially in the services and trades. The bus driver is simply "George," but one does not address Harvard University's president as "Drew," though for some reason the media called former President Clinton, "Bill" and the former First Lady, "Hillary."

I have been thinking about the meaning and nuances of names after discovering a little note in a farm memoir bought at a used bookstore. Called *Clabbered Dirt, Sweet Grass* and authored by Gary Paulsen, the slim volume is a poetic and powerful recreation of life on a farm of the high Middle West just as horse power was giving way to tractor power. It is my kind of book, so I resonated to the inscription made by the original purchaser: "Memories, for Dick from Pat, Christmas 1993."

I assumed that the book had been given by a loving wife to her husband, Dick, and in this frame of mind began reading. Then came a surprise. One evening a note fell out of the book that dampened the starry-eyed notion I had of Dick and Pat. The note read: "Richard, Fill the Wood box!" How the tone had changed! "Dick" had become "Richard"–more formal, almost commanding.

This August 22 my wife Jan and I will celebrate our 50h wedding anniversary. Never, if memory serves right, has my wife addressed me as "Milton" in five decades of marriage, though she has had reason to do so. Like Richard, I have not always, figuratively speaking, kept the wood box filled. When growing up there back in Iowa, I was always "Milton" but somehow after August 22, 1965, I became "Milt"–a token perhaps of the change in my status. Now I was husband, not son, and in my own household.

How is it with you and God? By what name are you spoken of in the heavenly councils? In Isaiah's time, the people of Israel, God's elect, had fallen upon hard times. Jerusalem was in ruins and Israel languished in captivity in Babylonia. The Jewish people had for too long ignored prophetic warnings against idolatry and empty rituals and had at last been given over to their enemies.

Then in Chapter 43 of Isaiah comes good news. The Holy One of Israel will remember those in far off Babylonia and bring them home. Indeed, Yahweh knows the captives by name. The work of deliverance is at hand. The Creator of the Universe ("unto me every knee shall bow, every tongue shall swear" 45:23) was calling the Israelites, forwarding them to freedom.

I find it a source of amazement that by Christian Baptism our names get recorded in the Book of Life. "Milton" is not a name I would have chosen for myself, as it has none of the luster of "Troy" or "Storm." When television came to my hometown in the 1950s, I was often called "Uncle Miltie"–with reference to a popular comedian of the day, Milton Berle.

I once asked mother as to why I was christened "Milton" and got the answer, "I'm not sure. It seemed like a nice name." Other kids were named after their grandfathers or great-grandfathers; I was given a name originally derived from Old English and referring to someone who came from a "mill town" or town with a mill!

Some people are so unhappy with their given names that they resort to the courts and take on new ones. Others hide embarrassing names and go by middle names or nicknames. My brother's wife's brother was given the name "Bruce" but became "Jack" to his friends–not so long a stretch, I suppose, for someone who went on to a professional career as the official national "Ronald McDonald." You've seen Bruce, alias Jack, alias Ronald, many times in commercials and on television–one of the few Lutherans I know who have led a successful double, no, triple life.

When the last trumpet sounds and the names from the Book of Life are read out, listen for your name. I plan to respond "It's me, it's me, O' Lord, Standing in the Need of Grace." I shall be thankful that on August 21, 1942, mother and father had me christened by the Rev. Gorge Koch and thereby enrolled as "Milton Charles" in the Book of Life. I am also thankful that mother was a nurse and that dad ran a gas station. Had they been of the prophetic caste, I might, like Isaiah's children, have been named either *Shear-jashub*, meaning "Remnant will return," or *Mahershalal-hash-baz*, meaning "Hasten booty, speed spoil."

September 2015

The Sweet Sleep of Labor

My wife and I decided that each of us would select a "do-nothing day" during which all the customary obligations of job and home would be set aside. My day came and I could not decide how to do nothing. Finally, in frustration, I ended up waterproofing the basement walls.

Psychologists tell us that there are bona fide workaholics for whom doing nothing is more emotionally wearing than the frenetic pace of the office or factory. At home they run from project to project as if merely puttering around was a sign of moral weakness.

Doing absolutely nothing comes hard for most of us. Even when at leisure we are careful not to appear indolent. The historian who reads historical novels on a weekday afternoon can always be said to be brushing up on professional skills as well as enjoying a good story. Vacationers come home more tired than when they left. Labor's holiday, the first Monday in September, is spent in one last pursuit of restoration through working at recreation.

Labor Day was first celebrated by the Knights of Labor in New York City in 1882. It reflected the growing challenge of workers' unions against an America dominated by the captains of industry and the idle rich.

Working with one's hands was honest labor; earning money on money, as the rich did, was less virtuous. Christian theologians once called such ill-gotten gain "usury" and praised instead the labors of those who earned their daily bread by the sweat of their brows. They looked to the writer of Ecclesiastes 5: 12 for justification: "The sleep of the laboring man is sweet, whether he eat little or much; but the abundance of the rich will not suffer him to sleep."

How do we apply this ethic to a society in which many Americans experience little of the hard physical labor of former generations and emotional rather than physical stress is a frequent complaint? No doubt there are many stopgap remedies. Some folks take up sports to offset the ills of a too sedentary job. Others, with doleful countenance, jog from here to there and sometimes back. Consultants cash in by offering stress management seminars for everyone from the clergy to air traffic controllers.

Henry Ward Beecher, the prominent 19th century preacher, had a much cheaper solution. Each evening he would retire to his basement and shovel the same pile of sand from one end to the other until exhausted and ready for a peaceful night's sleep.

Perhaps the solution lies not in more activity but in less. Try taking the Biblical command literally: "Six days thou shalt work, but on the seventh thou shalt rest." (Exodus 43:21) There is more here than remembering the Sabbath day to keep it holy.

Some of you may recall the time when after attending to worship, nothing but the most essential work was done on Sunday. Folks spent the day doing nothing at all. There were no Walmarts to go to and children did not rush off to the movies or to their friends' houses. Given the frenetic comings and goings in the typical home today, even on Sundays, it may be truthfully said that we no longer enjoy rest in the full Biblical sense.

Great composers use musical rests creatively, because rests define and give significance to the tones. Take the rests out of Handel's "Messiah" and you lose its musical beauty and powerful message.

A Sunday afternoon offers a "rest cure" from the disorders, physical, mental and spiritual, of daily life. The "sweet sleep of labor" mentioned in Ecclesiastes comes in realizing that work and rest are complimentary; each helps define and give meaning to the other.

Those of us raised on the notion that "idle hands are the devil's workshop" and doing nothing in particular is somehow sinful might well contemplate this Labor Day the benefits of what the English writer Thackeray called "dignified otiosity" (from the Latin *otiosus*, meaning leisure) and ponder the spiritual blessings implied in Walt Whitman's line, "I loaf and invite my soul."

October 2015

The Tablecloth

Some years ago I took a group of Syracuse University freshman to hear the always eloquent and moving Elie Wiesel, Nobel Prize winner for his witness to the world about the horrors of the Jewish Holocaust. A survivor himself, Wiesel wants the living to remember the millions who died when Fanaticism took on the name of Nazism and the innocent suffered. Our class read Wiesel's powerful narrative of his own imprisonment, called <u>Night</u>, and I attempted to impress upon students the need to build moral unity in a diverse society. Wiesel himself spoke of the requirement to be ever vigilant, so that the demons that gave rise to the Holocaust never again plague human history. I'm not entirely sure our discussion of Wiesel's book <u>Night</u> succeeded in helping students understand why it is important to remember the Holocaust. Perhaps I should have started with the following story, which was making the rounds on the Internet and is attributed to Pastor Rob Reid.

"The brand new pastor and his wife, newly assigned to their first ministry, to reopen a church in suburban Brooklyn, arrived in early October excited about their opportunities. When they saw their church, it was very run down and needed much work. They set a goal to have everything done in time to have their first service on Christmas Eve. They worked hard, repairing pews, plastering walls, painting, etc., and on Dec 18 were ahead of schedule and just about finished. On Dec 19 a terrible tempest -- a driving rainstorm -- hit the area and lasted for two days. On the 21st, the pastor went over to the church. His heart sank when he saw that the roof had leaked, causing a large area of plaster about 20 feet by 8 feet to fall off the front wall of the sanctuary just behind the pulpit, beginning about head high. The pastor cleaned up the mess on the floor, and not knowing what else to do but to postpone the Christmas Eve service, headed home.

On the way he noticed that a local business was having a flea market type sale for charity so he stopped in. One of the items was a beautiful, handmade, ivory colored, crocheted tablecloth with exquisite work, fine colors and a Cross-embroidered right in the center. It was just the right size to cover up the hole in the front wall. He bought it and headed back to the church. By this time, it had started to snow. An older woman running from the opposite direction was trying to catch the bus. She missed it. The pastor invited her to wait in the warm church for the next bus 45 minutes later. She sat in a pew and paid no attention to the pastor while he got a ladder, hangers, etc., to put up the tablecloth as a wall tapestry. The pastor could hardly believe how beautiful it looked and it covered up the entire problem area. Then he noticed the woman walking down the center aisle. Her face was white like a sheet. "Pastor," she asked, "where did you get that tablecloth?" The pastor explained. The woman asked him to check the lower right corner to see if the initials, EBG were crocheted into it there. They were. These were the initials of the woman, and she had made this tablecloth 35 years before in Austria.

The woman could hardly believe it as the pastor told how he had just gotten the Tablecloth. The woman explained that before the war she and her husband were well-to-do people in Austria. When the Nazis came, she was forced to leave. Her husband was going to follow her the next week. She was captured, sent to prison and never saw her husband or her home again. The pastor wanted to give her the tablecloth; but she made the pastor keep it for the church. The pastor insisted on driving her home; that was the least he could do. She lived on the other side of Staten Island and was only in Brooklyn for the day for a housecleaning job.

What a wonderful service they had on Christmas Eve. The church was almost full. The music and the spirit were great. At the end of the service, the pastor and his wife greeted everyone at the door and many said that they would return. One older man, whom the pastor recognized from the neighborhood, continued to sit in one of the pews and stare, and the pastor wondered why he wasn't leaving. The man asked him where he got the tablecloth on the front wall because it was identical to one that his wife had made years ago when they lived in Austria before the war and how could there be two tablecloths so much alike? He told the pastor how the Nazis came, how he forced his wife to flee for her safety, and he was supposed to follow her, but he was arrested and put in a prison. He never saw his wife or his home again in all the 35 years in between. The pastor asked him if he would allow him to take him for a little ride. They drove to Staten Island and to the same house where the pastor had taken the woman three days earlier. He helped the man climb the three flights of stairs to the woman's apartment, knocked on the door and he saw the greatest Christmas reunion he could ever imagine."

This month many Christians observe the Festival of the Reformation, marking the moment in history when Martin Luther struck a blow for Gospel freedom by nailing his 95 Theses on the door of the Castle Church of Wittenberg in 1517. Some 425 years later Elie Wiesel's family was sent to a concentration camp by agents of Nazi Germany, the same Germany out of which Luther came. When Hitler ruled Europe, Luther's legacy was in danger of being swept into the dustbin of history. How can the horrors of the death camps that Wiesel witnessed be reconciled with Luther's portrayal of a just and loving God? I don't have the answer and even Wiesel, a learned and pious man, struggled with how to give witness to the continuing humanity of God in the light of the inhumanity of man. We can only give voice to the good news of victory in Jesus the Christ.

Egg Money

Susan B. Anthony, the 19th-century women's rights leader, who hailed from Rochester, recalled that as a young girl she aspired to study mathematics in school. However, the male mathematics teacher, invoking traditional gender stereotypes about a woman's proper place, suggested that Susan ought to be content with studying her Bible and saving her egg money. Piety and frugality would make her a fitting candidate for marriage.

I have been thinking of the symbolic meaning of egg money as this Thanksgiving approaches. The customary image that Thanksgiving cards invoke is that of the overflowing cornucopia of harvest produce. Good things in abundance, a table groaning under the weight of turkey and pumpkin pie—that is the American way each Thanksgiving. However, what of the lean years when all a family has is but the equivalent of egg money to sustain the household? How is it possible to be thankful for blessings not received?

In the pre-1940 farm economy, almost all rural women kept poultry—chickens, ducks, or geese, but mostly chickens. Poultry work was woman's work, with the occasional help of the younger children. I recall that as late as the 1950s my Iowa aunts all had their chickens to feed and care for. In return, they always had eggs, some of which were taken into town for cash money. A farm woman's prized "egg money" was her own to do with as she saw fit, an independent source of income that many women used to buy groceries. Others salted it away for rainy day needs or to buy something extra for themselves or other family members. When hog and cattle prices went down and corn and oats died in the fields during the Dust Bowl and Great Depression years, the chickens kept on laying. There are many stories of how a farm wife dipped into her egg money to pay a doctor's bill or cover some other critical need when there was little else to sell or trade for hard cash.

One scholarly study of low-capital, non-quantified egg production as it existed before the emergence of today's mammoth mechanized egg and chicken factories (think Perdue) discovered that many farm women thought of money as something to use rather than count. As in the Biblical story of the widow's mite, their egg money was valuable not because it was much but because it could be rightly used—discretionary funds put to good purpose. In times such as ours, a person's worth is frequently determined by how much he or she earns. Some corporate chief executives take home salaries and bonuses that by any moral reasoning are excessive Big name athletes and celebrities command paychecks that border on the obscene. The pursuit of wealth has become the American obsession.

The observance of Thanksgiving affords all of us an opportunity rethink how we are using the blessings God has given us. Whether God has given us much or little is of no account, for it is in the giving that our own "egg money" takes on value. One informant in the study of Iowa poultry-raising told researchers that when he went to college and was barely scraping by, a letter would arrive from his mother in which a five-dollar bill had been tucked. The gift came, as you might guess, from his mother's small but precious reserve of "egg money." It was a token of love.

Perhaps it will do all of us well this Thanksgiving to think not of the overflowing cornucopia of good things so central to the American myth of perpetual abundance but of the beauty of not having except that which is truly needful. There is a long and honorable tradition in Christianity associated with the mendicant orders. The cowled monks went about bowl in hand, dependent on the charity of others. Except for staff, robe, and sandals, they had few possessions. They held to the belief that by ridding themselves of worldly things, they could achieve greater saintliness. Need we give away all that we have to the poor, as Jesus told the rich man in that most troubling New Testament passage, in order to enter into the Kingdom of God? In order to demonstrate our thankfulness to God, are we to divest ourselves of all that we have and become, like the monks of old, wandering beggars?

Perhaps the essential meaning of Jesus' words is that we should come to understand that true wealth is not in the having or the possessing but **in the use** of what material blessings come our way. Think then of your own cornucopia of Thanksgiving riches as "egg money"–safely put away for some good purpose one day. If your resources are running low this time year, look to keeping a few chickens.

December 2015

My Fiji Christmas

Some years back, the Sernett family was contemplating a Christmas without a tree. No Norway Spruce would grace the living room; no twinkling lights were to be strung and no ornaments put up. We planned to go to Texas for a family wedding and had decided to go treeless at home. In the interest of practicality, I suggested this radical change in Sernett family traditions, so have no cause to complain. Still, I was worried. Would Christmas be the same?

Having grown up in the Midwest, I have certain notions about what makes for an old-fashioned Christmas. Snow and an evergreen by the fireplace are essentials. Sentiment is a powerful force at this time of the year. It is said that we all revert to childhood memories in the presence of a bough of green cut from the forest and brought indoors. Preachers say that our celebration of Christ's birth ought to transcend these old customs. I know that they are right, but I was not sure that I would be able to handle a treeless holiday. So I put myself to a test. I dreamed of spending Christmas in Fiji, where there are no Norway Spruces, only coconut trees to hang your stockings on.

Beautiful white beaches, crystal clear lagoons, and the friendliest people anywhere! The travel brochures trumpet Fiji's archipelago of 330 islands as if they are anterooms to paradise itself. I saw myself on Christmas Day hiking up to volcanic peaks or angling for wahoo, marlin, and yellowfish tuna in the waters of Bega. Not a soul would be singing Bing Crosby's "White Christmas." Imagine my surprise at discovering that the good people of Fiji can manage to enjoy the holiday season without snow and the balsamed fir. Indeed, they seem to have kept the true spirit of the season more at the heart of their festivities than we here in the United States. Here is an example. On Christmas Day 2000, His Excellency Ratu Josefa Uluivuda Iloilo, MP, MBE, JP, issued a deeply spiritual message to the nation. I quote in part:

Ladies and Gentlemen, Young People and Children of Fiji.

The Joyful and Holy Season of Christmas is with Us Again. We Celebrate that Miraculous Moment 2000 Years ago when Jesus Christ, the Son of God, was Born in a Stable in Bethlehem. This Act of Divine Intervention Showed that God so Loved the World that He Sent it the Gift of His Only Son.

So Jesus Came and He Changed the World. He taught Us many Things in His Short Life. He Preached about Kindness, Forgiveness, Mercy and Humility. He Told Us to Help the Poor and All Those in Need. He wanted us to be Compassionate, Caring and Tolerant.

For Christians, the Message of Christmas has a Directedness that should not be Overlooked amidst the Celebrations, the Feasting and the Exchange of Presents. We have to Show that We are Worthy of the Gift God gave US in the Form of His Beloved Son—Not just in the Next Few Days but for the Rest of Our Lives.

We, in Fiji, of Whatever Origin, Belief or Religion Can Find Hope and Inspiration in All Those Teachings of Jesus. Our Country Descended into Darkness this Year. There was Evil at Work in the Land and It Caused Great Suffering. It Still Lurks in the Shadows.

What could this have meant? Was I not going to celebrate Christmas in a tropical paradise? It turns out that in June 2000 an armed group of ethnic Fijians staged a coup, invaded parliament and took Fiji's first ethnic Indian prime minister hostage. A newspaper account described the insurgents as "armed thugs asserting ethnic claims." Another report termed the coup "a grave setback for democracy and interracial relations." So much for my idyllic view of Christmas in Fiji.

When the Fiji coup took place fifteen years ago, we in the United States had little reason to fear evil lurking in the shadows in our own country. Now we have a Homeland Security Department and live in the post 9/11 age. My lamentations about a treeless Christmas seem beside the point.

I am driven to dwell on His Excellency's words about not overlooking the "Directedness" of the Message of Christmas. So let there be celebrations this year, filled with feasting and the exchange of presents, and, yes, even the tree if you must, but most of all, let us be worthy of **the Gift**.

January 2016

It's a Windy Day!

Each year about this time, the newspapers report stories about house fires. I have not made a statistical study of this phenomenon, but I am of the impression that fire fighters were called out a lot during the recent holiday season. Perhaps there are easy explanations--the widespread use in winter of portable heaters, defective Christmas tree lights, candles left burning, faulty fireplace flues, etc. We use our wood-burning fireplace more often these cold winter nights. I am paranoid about leaving it unattended.

Like the other basic elements—earth, wind, and water—fire has been interwoven into the human consciousness for as long as there have been humans. Without fire, we would have frozen up a long time ago. In one form or another, fire, which gives off both heat and light, has been the godmother of human civilization. Even as a lowly cub scout in the Wolf Pack many years ago, I would stare into the campfire and think (profoundly, I then believed) of the terrible and yet essential nature of fire. The same kind of flames that roasted my hotdog and toasted the marshmallows we all ate also burned down a farmer's barn, destroying his milk cows and his livelihood. Given this ghastly paradox, it is little wonder that I grew up confused at hearing devoutly religious people say that they were "on fire" with the Spirit of the Lord.

Lest I be misunderstood, we Lutherans back there in Iowa did not use the language of spiritual pyrotechnics. I suppose that Pentecostalists or some of those early camp meeting Methodists would have described us as lukewarm Christians—so temperate were we in our demonstrations of faith. It was upon leaving the Midwestern Lutheran fold that I encountered fellow believers who were both comfortable with the notion that the Holy Spirit is as much fire as wind and were not afraid to act fired up. This was especially the case in the African American religious traditions, rooted in traditional African practices and in American Southern "born again" evangelicalism, which I chose to study extensively. For some in these assemblies of believers, the Holy Spirit will not come without a Shout. In some Pentecostal traditions, "running to Jesus" requires such emotional and physical displays that all but the hardiest constitutions are broken down by the effort to get the Holy Spirit to descend.

While I respect those who can gain spiritual renewal by becoming "fired up" about Jesus, my own reading of Acts 2:1-4 leads me in a different direction. You know the story. Ten days after the Ascension of the one whom they now knew as the Son of God, Lord and Messiah, the disciples gathered in Jerusalem celebrating the first Pentecost. Suddenly, a mighty, rushing wind filled the assembly, a symbol of the presence and work of the Spirit of God. First came the wind; then came the fire or what appeared to be tongues of flame, descending upon the disciples as they gave witness to the wonder and glory of the story of Jesus in languages and dialects not known to them. Some Christians have adopted fire as the primary symbol of the Holy Spirit at work. Here in upstate New York, religious revivals led by the evangelist Charles G. Finney were so intense in the 1820s, sweeping back and forth across the region, that the central and western portions are called "The Burned-over District." I know, too, of a group of believers who call themselves "fire-baptized" Christians.

You may think it small potatoes to argue that wind is a better symbolic representation of the Spirit of God than fire, especially for New Testament Christians. Here is my reasoning. Wind, not fire, is there at the beginning when God creates. The Book of Genesis speaks about God breathing the "breath of life" into Adam. In the Hebrew, the word for spirit also means breath. Fire, by way of contrast, is at the end—Hell is traditionally described as a fiery, not a windy place. And when our personal "fourscore and ten" allotment runs out, we exhale our last breath, not a plume of flame. Medieval Christians equated this "last breath" with the flight of the soul from earth to heaven. Pit fire against wind, and wind always wins. Without wind, or air, fire ceases to be.

Perhaps I have become partial to wind because our house is set up on a ridge where the wind blows and blows. Across the valley up Fenner way, twenty windmills turn day in and day out. In a pinch, we could generate heat and light from wind. I like to listen for the wind on a still and quiet day, particularly on a sultry summer's night when the first currents of a cooling wind stir up off the pond across the road. But one has to listen, really listen, as if one's very existence depends on catching the first signs of a change in the flow and dance of subatomic particles.

Isn't this also the way it is with the voice of God? One needs to block out all of those distracting noises that characterize life today. Everywhere we go there is noise, annoying noise—in elevators, restaurants, hospitals, yes, even church. It is good to be quiet and to listen as you have never listened before. Do you hear what I hear? If so, go out into the wind, Pooh-bear like, trusting the adventure of it all.

February 2016

Where's Your Comfort Blanket?

When the thermometer plunges, wise folks throw on another blanket or two. My wife has made more than a dozen blankets for family and friends from fleece that she purchases at JoAnn Fabrics. One "throw" went to a nephew and his wife who were expecting their first child. Another went to a good friend recovering from surgery. I remember Jan cutting and tying a green and white blanket for our sister-in-law, who recently took a nasty fall after slipping on the ice. I am happy to say that I was not left out. Jan made me a "throw" to supplement the warmth of our pellet stove these cold nights. My blanket, appropriately enough, is festooned with images of John Deere tractors. I am not embarrassed to say that I will hang onto it until it is reduced to tatters, a few threads of comfort.

Perhaps you had a "comfort blanket" when you were a child. It went wherever you went, and as you grew older, your parents worried some that you would still be clinging to the thing when you went off to college. A child expert once offered this remedy for separating youngsters from their favorite security blanket: Cut it

175

in half the first day, and repeat this procedure daily until the blanket is a one-inch square!

I read this so-called expert's solution in a marvelous collection of miscellanea entitled Gleanings: The Ultimate Scrapbook by the Rev. Graham R. Hodges. Born in 1915 in the little town of Wesson, Mississippi, Hodges attended Yale Divinity School and thereafter served Congregational churches in Ticonderoga, Crown Point, and, from 1956 to 1979, in Watertown. A prolific author, essayist, and writer of editorials, Hodges was an activist clergyman, offering comfort to many a troubled soul while working for the improvement of the communities in which he lived.

Hodges was battling cancer and had been given only a few months to live when I first met him. I went to visit Hodges at his apartment in the Greenpoint complex in Liverpool. His abode overflowed with books and assorted ephemera, an indication that his life-long packrat propensities continued. Well wishers dropped by, and his son, a historian friend of mine, was there to help him sort out his affairs. Our conversation touched on a variety of topics; there is hardly an issue of importance about which the Rev. Hodges lacked an informed opinion. Even as he confronted the prospect of his own demise, this man of faith was fiercely interested in the welfare of others. He was the definitive free man—expressing his opinions without any fear of what people might think of him. He told me that no one is as free to speak on controversial issues of the day than a retired Congregational clergyman who is dying. Before we parted company, he autographed a copy of his book Gleanings (which runs to 400 pages or so) for me.

I came across a short musing about "Comfort Blankets" in Hodges' scrapbook. There is no belittling of what Hodges calls "cuddle blankets"—however irrational, for they give us comfort and strength for the night (or day). Hodges points out that many an adult cannot function without having a cup of coffee the first thing in the morning. He argues that as long as something is not addictive or destructive in some way, there is nothing inherently wrong with having your own personal "comfort blanket."

Rev. Hodges spent a lifetime telling the comfortless about the ultimate "Comfort Blanket." His scrapbook collection rings with a confident faith. No matter how rocky the road, the promise of Jesus stands. "In my father's house are many mansions. If this were not so, I would have told you. I go to prepare a place for you." Hodges asks "What more do we need?"

I was impressed with the sterling faith and sharp intellect of this aging (and dying) witness for the Lord. I told his son that it's too bad that there aren't more people like the Rev. Graham Hodges in this world—decent, caring, and courageous. His son (as sons are wont to do when you cast their fathers as heroic icons), responded, "He's not God." No, the Rev. Graham Hodges was not God, but God had called him by name and wrapped him in the ultimate comfort blanket of divine love. That makes all the difference in this cold world.

"And what does the Lord require of you, but to do justice and to love kindness and to walk humbly with your God."
Micah 6:8

March 2016

The Voice of the Turtle Dove on Easter Morning

At the March writing of this, the long winter's accumulation of snow and ice still covers the ground. With brooding spirit we've longed for that first fresh sign of the renewal of green and growing things. The Psalm from the Songs of Solomon (2: 12) is on our lips: "For, the winter is past, the rain is over and gone; the singing of birds is at hand and the voice of the turtle is heard in our land." Surely you think, the poet is mistaken: turtles do not sing (beetles yes, turtles no).

Actually, "the voice of the turtle" refers to a Persian wild cousin of our dove with the name tur-tur, from which turtledove is derived. Noted in the Old World for their plaintive cooing, turtledoves are popularly called mourning doves (*Zanaidura macrou*ra). Resembling miniature passenger pigeons, grey in color and common throughout the United States, they travel as far south as Panama in the winter. But with the arrival of spring, the mourning doves return to our neighborhoods, harbingers of the advancing season of renewal and new birth.

For many years I mistakenly thought this doleful but comforting bird to be a morning dove, associating it with those sunny mornings after a spring night rain had cooled the hot Midwestern prairie. Just after dawn and before the noise of the day, one could hear the cooing love song of the male dove, with its note of tender sadness.

But now I understand why the turtle dove is so frequently associated in religious art and literature with the Christ story--for it is not only a morning song one hears but a mournful one, the low, continuous lament of the dove for its beloved.

Christians grieve on Good Friday when the book is closed and we are confronted with the bitter fruit of our sin. We sorrow at the loss of the Righteous One, now laid in the tomb hewn out of rock--the One whom even the Roman centurion said, "Truly, this man was the Son of God!" Darkness surrounds us and we put on the garments of those who mourn. But upon the dawn of Easter Morning, we arise to sing a New Song.

"Forth he came at Easter, like the risen grain, He that for three days in the ground had lain, Raised from the Dead, my Living Lord is seen; Love is come gain like wheat arising green."

All the world over, from the ancient Abbey at Mont-Saint-Michel on a rock 164 feet high and half mile in diameter in the Gulf of St. Malo (France) to the ramshackle one-room church of the Living God and Pillar of Truth in rural Georgia, Christians turn from mourning the coldness of death to celebrating with glad Hosannas! the morning of their salvation.

Indeed, the expression "Hosanna!" is derived from the Hebrew and means "save, we pray." Or as a young contributor to Children's Letters to God put it, "Dear God, Count me in! Your friend, Herbie." Yes, we too say, "Count us in, O Lord, let us share in the good news, "HE IS RISENl HE IS RISEN, IN-DEED!"

And so we are moved to sing with the hymnist not of death and darkness but of life and love:

Now the green blade rises from the buried grain,
Wheat that in dark many days has lain,
Love lives again, that with the dead has been.
Love is come again like wheat arising green.

April 2016

Celestial Humor

Mark Twain, wise and witty at the same time, once wrote: "The secret source of humor itself is not joy but sorrow. There is no humor in heaven." Twain's comment, irreverent though it might be, points to a fundamental paradox in the Easter story we heard about last month and in the human experience. As the great comedians will tell you, humor is a way of dealing with pain, yes, even sorrow. Remove the pain and the need for diversion and escape through laughter is removed. That is why Twain can say that Heaven, a state of perpetual bliss, is humorless. Whoever heard of angels laughing!! But if "being with God" means to be without laughter, then where is the joy! It is indeed a paradox.

Red Skelton (whom I used to refer to as "Red Skeleton" in the 1950s and 1960s when his TV show aired weekly in our household) defined "funny" for a whole generation. Who can forget "Freddie Freeloader," the mute hobo clown, or the dim-witted "Clem Kadiddlehopper," another of Skelton's alter egos. Then there was the inebriated "Cauliflower McPugg" and the sad-sack "Willie Lump-Lump." We laughed at Red Skelton, who died at the age of 84 in 1997 after an extended illness, not so much because he told "jokes." No, we laughed because his routines, his characters, reminded us of ourselves.

Skeleton used humor to strip away artifice and pretense, just as a good preacher does by holding up God's Law as a mirror to our lives. Laughter is our safety valve, our way of acknowledging that we have fallen short of the mark, that, when all is said and done, all that we strive to build up in this life will turn to dust, even our mortal selves. Which reminds me of the following funny story, sometimes attributed to Skeleton, whose life was by no means without pain and sorrow—thrice married (and divorced), jilted of money by his so-called friends and advisors, angry about his show being cancelled in 1971:

After church, Johnny tells his parents he has to go and talk to the minister right away. They agree and the pastor greets the family.

"Pastor," Johnny says, "I heard you say today that our bodies came from the dust."

"That's right, Johnny, I did."

"And I heard you say that when we die, our bodies go back to dust."

"Yes, I'm glad you were listening. Why do you ask?"

"Well you better come over to our house right away and look under my bed 'cause there's someone either comin' or goin'!"

The good news proclaimed on that first Easter morning is that the "last laugh" (a loud cosmic hurrah!) belongs to Christians who recognize in the resurrection of Jesus a final triumph over all pain and sorrow. At Christmastime, we knelt in silent, awesome wonder with the shepherds before the manger that held Mary's child, both baby and the King of Kings. Easter, by way of contrast, was and is a noisy celebration of the culmination of the church year and of that ancient and yet very contemporary story of God's love incarnate.

March seemed early for Easter and to have it precede April Fool's Day (April 1) seems especially odd this year. When I was young, April Fool's Day meant getting up early and trying to play a trick on my younger siblings, such as telling my brother that someone had stolen his bike, whereupon he would jump out of bed and rush to the garage in a state of great alarm, only to find that I had stashed his bike under the porch (I had an undeveloped sense of humor).

Though the origin of April Fool's Day itself is uncertain, Mark Twain said this about its purpose: "The first of April is the day we remember what we are the other 364 days of the year." Lest you think Twain is here rendering God's handiwork no complement, consider this bit of Twain lore. With a twinkle in his eye, the man from Hannibal, Missouri, also said: "Ah well, I am a great and sublime fool. But then I am God's fool, and all His works must be contemplated with respect."

Recognizing oneself as one of God's fools (great and sublime, despite all) is the divine spark found in our ongoing Easter faith.

May 2016

In Memorium

The month of May holds two strong memories for me. School let out in Iowa as Memorial Day approached when I was young. This meant no more teacher's rules and homework until after Labor Day. For those of us in the High School Band, May was the month to march out to the Hampton Cemetery where the community held a brief ceremony to honor local residents who had given  their lives in defense of our country. We donned our band uniforms and white buck shoes for one last time, fell in line behind the flag bearers, played a few patriotic tunes, and, despite Mr. Freeze's orders, broke rank to scramble after the shell casings that flew about when the honor guard fired a salute over the cemetery pond.

I have participated in Memorial Day observances in New England and in Upstate New York, and have remarked on how common and comfortable the rituals are. Scholars of American religion tell us that Memorial Day, like July 4th, is a hallmark of our national civil religion, a ritual that transcends denominational and sectarian differences and instructs us about being "Americans." Choose your community, especially in small town America, and I will show you bands marching, preachers praying, politicians orating, and flags flying. As a boy of 14, I enjoyed Hampton's effort to create a collective feeling of respect and reverence for those who went off to fight on some foreign field and never returned. I liked the sound and fury of it all, the display of color, and, yes, the theater. The sight of W. W. I veterans, fewer with each passing year, raising bony hands to salute the flag touched me, while the recollection of W. W. II veterans stuffing themselves into uniforms that no longer fit still brings a smile.

The Memorial Days of my youth were usually sunny and bright. School was out, and we marched along in a grand almost giddy manner. We were, after all, young and immortal. We clarinetists had the tricky passages of John Philip Sousa's marches down pat. We had nothing to fear as we entered the cemetery gates and wound our way up to the knoll where carpenters had erected a wooden platform the previous night.

A half hour later our mood had changed, at least mine usually did. It has taken me some time to understand this transformation. Only recently have I located the source of my discomfiture. She always sat in the shadow of the male politicians, military officers, and preachers. She had no role to play in the festivities until it came time to present her with a folded United States flag. She was called "The Gold Star Mother." In those years a "Gold Star Mother" was a local woman whom the authorities had selected to honor because she had lost a son in one of the World Wars or the Korean War. We had no "Gold Star Fathers," though I am sure that fathers grieved just as much as mothers over the death of those to whom they had given life. Perhaps because men made wars, they felt it necessary to give women this small part in Memorial Day observances.

Now that my mother lays at rest not far from the knoll where we honored Hampton's "Gold Star Mothers," I can understand why I usually left the cemetery with some thing gnawing at my youthful spirits. I was not yet of draft age, but had I been the Selective Service Bureau might have called my number and sent me off to a place of death, and mother would have had no recourse but to watch, and wait, and then weep--just as the "Gold Star Mothers" did. What does the month of May mean to a Gold Star Mother? How do you reconcile Mother's Day and Memorial Day for her?

All of this came home to me when I was far away from home visiting the Scottish National War Memorial in Edinburgh Castle, Scotland. Opened by the Prince of Wales in 1927, the War Memorial was designed to honor the laddies who died during the Great War of 1914-18. Like most tourists, we were pressed for time, so I could only page through the memorial books that listed each Scottish soldier, his place of birth and place of death. From farms and villages Scotland's youth went off to die, often in places they and their parents had never heard of. I knew none of the names inscribed in this book of the dead, yet I felt that same tug at the heart I had known when leaving the cemetery after Hampton's Memorial Day many years ago. "The Gold Star Mother" is a universal figure. A Scottish mother and an American mother on Memorial Day walk the cemetery in need of no cultural translator. When they cry, they cry a universal language.

Neither Memorial Day nor Mother's Day are church festivals. We have no rituals, no readings, no theologies specific to May's special days. And yet, we Christians, if we are true to the centrality of the teachings of Jesus, should focus on the "Theology of the Cross," not the "Theology of Glory." Every "Gold Star Mother" reminds us to temper the rhetoric of glory that puffs up a nation, making war seem sane. There are no good wars, no good deaths--save one. The "Theology of the Cross" teaches us that if we are to glory, we do so not in "the might of arms" but in Him who wore a Crown of Thorns, in Christ Jesus, the King of Kings who died on a cross.

Roots and Reunions

Summertime is the season for family reunions. The ancestral hornpipe sounds across our nation, calling the scattered clan together. In ancient times of memory (the 1950s to me), most of the Sernett, Berghoefer, Dorow, and Boehnke tribe lived within an easy drive of each other. Nothing was very structured. No one consulted the Family Reunion Institute at Temple University for ideas on what to do or eat. Aunts and Uncles, Brothers and Sisters, and Cousins by the carload got together simply because we were kin. We had lots of fried chicken, sweet corn (if the raccoons hadn't beat us to it), Kool-Aid for the kids and beer for the grown-ups (men, mostly). And there was talk—lots of talk, mostly about crops and weather, church gossip, and what the kids and grandkids were up to. I didn't truly appreciate the ritual of it all, the sacredness of those old reunions--at the time. I was having too much fun. Today I look at my mother's photo album pictures of those family gatherings and marvel at how God uses the family tree (root, trunk, branch and twig) as a channel of grace. Family reunions are sacramental events.

Now it is much more difficult to experience that grace. Our tribe is scattered across the land, as no doubt your extended family is. We have to work at getting together—juggling calendars and travel plans. In this age of email and cell phones, the traditional family reunion is an endangered species. That is why I am looking forward to a gathering of my family/clan/tribe in Osage, Iowa, this July 4th weekend. Most of my cousins are now in their 70s, some in their 80s. All of my mother's generation is gone. There is a new crop of grandchildren (those twigs), but they may not fully appreciate the sacredness of the event. As one gets older, genealogy (your own genealogy) takes on greater significance than it did when you were young and focused on the moment.

The Bible, especially the Old Testament, is a genealogical treasure trove of the first order. I used to find reading about all those "begats" mind-numbing when we studied them in Sunday school. Now I understand something of their importance. Look at the opening verses of the Gospel of Matthew:

1.   1:1 The book of the generation of Jesus Christ, the son of David, the son of Abraham.

2.   1:2 Abraham begat Isaac; and Isaac begat Jacob; and Jacob begat Judas and his brethren; 1:3 And Judas begat Phares and Zara of Thamar; and Phares begat Esrom; and Esrom begat Aram; 1:4 And Aram begat Aminadab; and Aminadab begat Naasson; and Naasson begat Salmon; 1:5 And Salmon begat Booz of Rachab; and Booz begat Obed of Ruth; and Obed begat Jesse; 1:6 And Jesse begat David the king; and David the king begat Solomon of her that had been the wife of Urias; 1:7 And Solomon begat Roboam; and Roboam begat Abia; and Abia begat Asa; 1:8 And Asa begat Josaphat; and Josaphat begat Joram; and Joram begat Ozias; 1:9 And Ozias begat Joatham; and Joatham begat Achaz; and Achaz begat Ezekias; 1:10 And Ezekias begat Manasses; and Manasses begat Amon; and Amon begat Josias; 1:11 And Josias begat Jechonias and his brethren, about the time they were carried away to Babylon: 1:12 And after they were brought to Babylon, Jechonias begat Salathiel; and Salathiel begat Zorobabel; 1:13 And Zorobabel begat Abiud; and Abiud begat Eliakim; and Eliakim begat Azor; 1:14 And Azor begat Sadoc; and Sadoc begat Achim; and Achim begat Eliud; 1:15 And Eliud begat Eleazar; and Eleazar begat Matthan; and Matthan begat Jacob; 1:16 And Jacob begat Joseph the husband of Mary, of whom was born Jesus, who is called Christ.

The "begetting" in the Old Testament prepared the way for Jesus, son of Joseph and Mary. Matthew is telling us that Christ, our Lord and Savior, has a family history—a royal lineage. Jesus has roots; he was not combusted out of thin air—an interloper on this planet from who knows where. To know him is to know his father, and his father's father, etc. So it is with us. God gave us families so that we can say to the world, "I belong."

They are almost all gone now—those orphanages that used to dot our land. However, they are reminders that not everyone belongs, even to this day. The Rev. and Mrs. J. G. Lemen founded The Christian Home Children's Orphanage at Council Bluffs, Iowa, in 1882 for orphaned children between the ages of 2 and 15. They began with six children but by 1910 were caring for nearly 100. I look at the 1910 census for Kane Township and think of those children who were unlikely to ever experience the joys of a family reunion. Whatever happened to Stella Cowles, 12 yr. 8 mo., born in Iowa? Did little Harold Madden, only 1 month old, ever find out who begat him or look up his genealogy? Then there is Hester Laub living in an orphanage at the age of 32! Her "brothers and sisters" are all un-related fellow orphans. Her "parents," as it were, are the Lemans. But the Rev. Lemen and his good wife have so many to look after. Did they remember to bake her a birthday cake? Or give her a hug when she did well in school? Perhaps they did. Perhaps Hester found happiness in her orphanage family. Maybe she even left the home and its dorms to go out into the world and have a family of her own. Let us imagine too that the orphanage held annual "family reunions" for all the scattered flock who left the care of the Lemens.

Family reunion season is a good time to remember that you have two genealogical identities. One is your biological family tree (your begats); the other is your family of faith, which is there for you in season and out. No matter how orphaned you might feel or where you are located on your ancestral chart, you have a superior citizenship. By Baptism, you belong to the family of God.

July 2016

Keeping Cool

Mother frowned upon air conditioning, believing it symptomatic of moral weakness. At the very least, it was a frivolous expense. My siblings and I suffered through many a hot and humid Iowa summer. When the humidity and temperature became intolerable, we sought refuge in the basement. The concrete-block pit upon which our house sat was cool and damp. One could get pneumonia by sleeping down in the cellar, but, given a choice, we took the risk. Better to sleep in the dank cellar than toast in the ovens our small bedrooms became when the tropical heat held Iowa in its grip.

Health officials remind us to ward off heat stroke by staying out of the direct sun and drinking plenty of liquids. Had I a dime for every can of soda Americans will consume this month, I could retire to Alaska. When the sun is hot enough to fry the proverbial egg, the pop (a Midwestern version of soda) machines do a land office business. I have a theory that one can tell much about the character of a person when they are thirsty and approach one of these mechanical devices for delivering (at a price) life-sustaining fluids. Station yourself near a drink vending machine in any public place. The more cantankerous the machine, the better. Now watch the body language of the desperate.

The pop dispensing device in Old Main, a male dormitory at Concordia College, St. Paul, Minnesota, in the early 1960s, had a personality of its own. A mechanism, always unruly, dropped a cup onto a metal grid. The machine was then to shoot a stream of pop into the cup. More often than not, students put a quarter in and nothing happened. These would-be preachers and teachers reacted in various ways. Some boxed and kicked the inanimate object in front of them. The soda machine was so dented one would have thought it had been dropped from a B-27 bomber during W.W. II. Others kept their physical cool but let go such a torrent of verbal abuse that my meager cussing vocabulary was considerably enriched. I had not realized with what creativity my classmates could swear. Old Main's pop machine revealed the true character of those who sought its refreshing liquors, more so than any standard personality test.

One afternoon long ago, I happened to be at the end of the hallway in which this infernal box stood when in came our professor of Greek New Testament. Faculty rarely appeared in the dormitories, so we suspected only the greatest of thirsts had brought him inside Old Main. Knowing how thoroughly we had been tested by that pop machine, we watched with nervous anticipation as this respected professor put in his quarter. I don't think he knew we were eyeing him from a distance, so what happened next was totally genuine, and to me astounding. I feared the worst. What if he swore a blue streak and flailed at the machine uncontrollably? Would we lose all respect for him and never be able to master biblical Greek? In went the quarter. Down swished the live-giving liquid. But no cup had dropped!! Professor Middleton's soda gurgled down the drain. In the next moment, this Christian gentleman taught us more about keeping our cool than any lecture. He watched bemusedly as the soda disappeared, said simply, "Well, look at that," turned on his heel and walked calmly out the door.

My roommates and I were awestruck. This was contrary to all we knew about human nature on a hot day. Where did a man get such strength of character, such power over the animal Id that is in all of us? I know not what the other twenty-year olds drew from this lesson in self-control, but I have been searching for the source of Prof. Middleton's "coolness" ever since. I did not have the courage more than fifty years ago to pay my respects at his office in order to solicit his philosophy of life. I suspect he would have pointed me to the very book that we fledgling biblical scholars were attempting to read in its original languages.

Check out the Bible and you will discover that thirst is a metaphor for the state of sin. Jesus says in John 7. 37, "If any thirst, let him come unto me and drink." Christ is spoken of as the source of "living waters" --surely a powerful image in an area of Palestine where near desert conditions can exist. Maybe this was Prof. Middleton's wellspring of coolness.

August 2003

On Why There Are No Cell Phones in Heaven

I was mystified the other day by a strange small beeping sound. I did not want to close up the house while the origin of that high-pitched "beep" went unresolved. The strange sound might signal imminent disaster, so I ran through the house checking out the usual suspects–computers, microwaves, fire alarms, etc. The beeping seemed loudest in my study, but when I walked into the kitchen, I heard it there. Maybe it was something in the basement, so down I went. Beep! Beep! Still, I could not locate the cause. This was maddening. The sound seemed to emanate from each nook and cranny of our house, but I could not pinpoint it. In frustration, I decided to leave. If the house burned down or something exploded, I at least could tell my wife that I had done my best. As I opened the car door to get in, the mystery was resolved. That beeping sound was emanating from me, or, to be more precise, from the cell phone in my pocket. The poor thing's battery was low and wanted attention.

Veteran cell phone users are no doubt laughing at my naiveté. I still use an old flip phone and have no cell phone contract. I grew up in a time when aunts and uncles had those old-style wall phones and a lady sat at the switchboard. My mother rarely made a long distance call. I think poorly of cell phone users I see who use the instrument for trivial pursuits–they chatter with friends about inane matters while I stand behind them in the line at the postal counter or call home while at the grocery store to find out what kind of toothpaste grandma likes. Overall, I consider the cell phone a necessary evil.

The theological meaning of the concept of "a necessary evil" is hard to explain. How, if God is a god of the good, can something be both necessary for us and evil at the same time? Is the concept akin to what a mother tells a sick child while spooning cod liver oil down the sufferer's throat? On the other hand, is it more like sleep–too little of it and one cannot function; too much time in bed, and one risks being labeled a slacker. Moderation is the solution to the sleep problem. However, the sick child needs enough of the bitter tasting medicine to make the little one well–moderation will not do. I am thinking that the theologians would tell us that a necessary evil does not come to us in moderate dosages. We hurt in order that we can receive some benefit. It is a peculiar moral equation.

Christians of all persuasions have resorted to the concept of "necessary evil" in their attempt to sort out the contradictions of life. War has been termed a "necessary evil," as has the resort to violence in cases of self-protection. Abortion advocates sometimes speak of it as a "necessary evil," and several of the classical theological-philosophers, such as Aquinas, wrote of prostitution as necessary social function albeit it evil one in a world ruled by human passion. The Puritans thought of sex as evil, but necessary for procreation. Idealists whose utopian dreams have faltered acknowledge government as unavoidable. Talk to your neighbor who loves to fish and hunt all year round, and he will tell you that work is for him something he dislikes but necessary nevertheless.

How do we make sense of all of this? The tendency in our times is to diminish individual responsibility by categorizing all that is burdensome to ourselves or our neighbors (including the global community in instances of ecological sin) as necessary evils about which we can do nothing. Our cars pollute, but so what, we have to get to work. It seems to me that we need to get back to the Biblical definition of sin. Sin is something that we choose to do as creatures gifted with free will. It does no one moral good to categorize something as a "necessary evil" when we have the power to alter the circumstances. Some of my University colleagues spoke of our administrators (deans, vice-chancellors and such) as "necessary evils" fettering their lives. These same critics were, of course, very happy to receive research awards from a dean whom they privately dismissed as an impediment at best and a useless bureaucrat at worst.

How is it in your life? Do you complain of this or that "necessary evil"–something or someone who makes your days miserable? If there is a lesson to be learned from my experience with that Verizon cell phone, it is this. Find the source of your discontent and do something about it. It may be that your perceived "evil" is neither necessary nor, wonder of wonders, bad in and of itself. My solution has been to turn off the cell phone so that its battery cannot run low and it will not have to beep for attention. I rarely take the cell phone with me when out and about, a solution that you might think silly. What, you ask, is the purpose of having a cell phone if you do not have it with you or make use of it? Now that I reflect on the matter more seriously, a cell phone is not a necessity. I got along fine without one for the first sixty years of my life.

As Christians, we stand "betwixt and between," susceptible to all of the troubles of this world. Yet, we are also a people of Promise. When fully translated into inhabitants of that heavenly City of God, we shall be freed of all evils–necessary or otherwise. Then we will understand that there is but one necessary good and that is to glorify God.

September 2016

Home Schooling

My cousin Winton loves pecans, and so do the squirrels in his back yard down there in Lubbock, Texas. Therein lies an ethical dilemma--too few pecans to make pecan pie and keep the squirrels happy at the same time. Getting rid of the squirrels is easier said than done, short of poisoning them or shooting them. Winton is a peace-loving and gentle man who spent his younger years helping German refugees from Communism's takeover of Eastern Europe after WW II. Most of his professional life has been in service to Native Americans under the auspices of the Bureau of Indian Affairs, and he had a career with the Social Security Administration. Killing pecan-robbing squirrels, or anything else for that matter, is not in his nature. What to do?

This month millions of children will enter the American school system. Most arrive on the doorstep of public education with fragile and often fuzzy notions of right and wrong. Some come with moral consciences informed not by loving parents or solid religious instruction but by a too rich diet of Saturday morning cartoons, where questions of right and wrong are resolved by a punch in the nose. Our adult world is no less confusing. No wonder American teenagers engaged in unhealthy behavior (ranging from the abuse of drugs to the exploitation of their own bodies) justify their actions by pointing to the hypocrisy of adults.

In the thick of this moral chaos it is increasingly difficult for those who have been baptized into Christ to conform to the Biblical standards set forth in the Ten Commandments, not to mention the 'higher law" of love Jesus taught and modeled in his earthly ministry. It is not enough (remember the story of the rich young man) to say, "I have not stolen today." The divine judge will ask, "Have you given to the poor today?" The task before us is to move forward in life without falling into ethical literalism, where the letter of the law becomes more powerful than the spirit, or sliding into situation ethics that allows for anything if justified by the context. Approach A to choosing right from wrong places Law over Gospel. Approach B robs the Law of its proper intent and thereby undercuts the power of the Gospel.

How to find living space (to act and to do) between "A" and "B" is the difficult lesson of life, something we start to learn as children (yes, even in kindergarten) and must embrace as continuing education all of our lives. If we get stuck in option "A," we can end up like those anti-meat protestors who vilify the Oscar Meyer Weenie wagon. If we adopt option "B" as the guiding philosophy of life, we have no moral high ground to criticize the cannibal, not to mention folks in the Philippines to whom a "hot dog" was once a canine. Somehow we need to find a middle way.

My cousin Winton demonstrated how to do this in his solution to the squirrel problem. I have a photo showing Winton with one of those large water guns kids use on hot summer days. He (gently) "blasts" the squirrels out of the pecan trees, captures them in wire cages, and then transports them off his property. My brother Gil (a recent visitor) tells me that Winton, a cleaver man, though he be a good Christian, gives the squirrels a little ride, taking them across a busy highway and letting them scamper into the scrub land. Now if the pesky critters get a hankering for Winton's pecans, they cross a super highway and contend with the sixteen-wheelers barreling across the Texas high country.

Perhaps Winton learned how to balance out two goods (save the squirrels and enjoy a slice of pecan pie) from his mother, my Aunt Martha. I can recall how Aunt Martha resolved the issue of prayer before meals. At home I was taught to pray before every meal and when about age seven thought this meant I had to "thank Jesus" at every visit to the drinking fountain in Franklin Elementary. Aunt Martha was not such a quibbler; she could not afford to be one on the Dorow farm where a large family was constantly popping in and out of her kitchen for snacks. Therefore, she made up a rule (a dispensation extended to visiting nieces and nephews). We did not need to pray unless there were more than three items (not counting drinks) on the table. We learned gratitude and charity at the same time. I hope that the homes and schools of America still contain the likes of Aunt Martha, who instilled in all of her children respect for Law and Gospel.

Dr. Milt Sernett

About the Author

Dr. Milton C. Sernett (b. 1942) grew up in Hampton, Iowa. He attended Concordia College, St. Paul, 1961-62 before transferring to the Senior College at Ft. Wayne, Indiana. He is a graduate of Concordia Seminary, St. Louis, Missouri, (M.Div. 1968), and received the M. A. & Ph.D. in American History from the University of Delaware (1969; 1972. He joined the faculty of Syracuse University in 1975 after teaching church history for three years at Concordia Theological Seminary, Springfield, Illinois. Sernett is currently Professor Emeritus of African American Studies and of History and Adjunct Professor of Religion at Syracuse University. His principal areas of teaching and research have been African American religious history, the American South, the abolitionist movement, the Underground Railroad, and American social reform movements.

Sernett was a Research Fellow at the W.E.B. Du Bois Institute, Harvard University, in 1988-89. In 1994-95 he was a Fulbright Senior Scholar at the John F. Kennedy Institute for North American Studies, Free University, Berlin, Germany. He is on the Cabinet of Freedom of the National Abolition Hall of Fame and Museum, Peterboro, New York. Sernett joined the emeriti ranks of Syracuse University faculty on May 15, 2005. He continues to teach an online Underground Railroad course and a course on the history of American abolitionism during his retirement.

Sernett has published seventeen books and numerous scholarly essays. Among his books are the classic text <u>African American Religious History: A Documentary Witness</u>; <u>North Star Country: Upstate New York and the Crusade for African American Freedom</u>, and <u>Harriet Tubman: Myth, Memory, & Freedom</u>. Sernett has also published books on topics as diverse as a history of cheesemaking, the transition from horsepower to tractors on

American farms, and a study of the origin of the Holstein breed of dairy cattle. His book <u>Farm</u> focuses on changes in American farming in New York State using the life of the master farmer Jared Van Wagenen, Jr., of Schoharie County. Sernett has also published a book on his German-American heritage and on his Bohemian (Czech) American heritage.

Sernett received the Distinguished Africanist Award from the New York African Studies Association in 2009. He received the Honorary Doctor of Letters degree from Concordia University, St. Paul, Minnesota at the graduation ceremonies on May 13, 2011.

Milt Sernett and his wife Jan live on Ridge Road north of Cazenovia. They began attending the Cazenovia United Methodist Church in 2011. They became associate members in 2013.

Made in the USA
Middletown, DE
16 May 2016